Donovan

Reading Success

Book 6

By
Celia Stone, Elizabeth Franks, & Myra Nicholson

Cover Design by
Terri Moll

Inside Illustrations by
Valery Larson

Publisher
LDA
a division of Instructional Fair Group
a Tribune Education Company
Grand Rapids, Michigan 49544

LDA

LDA grants the right to the individual purchaser to reproduce patterns and student activity materials in this book for noncommercial individual or classroom use only. Reproduction for an entire school or school system is strictly prohibited. No other part of this publication may be reproduced in whole or in part. No part of this publication may be reproduced for storage in a retrieval system, or transmitted in any form or by any means, electronic, mechanical, recording, or otherwise, without the prior written permission of the publisher. For information regarding permission write to: LDA, Instructional Fair Group, P.O. Box 1650, Grand Rapids, MI 49501.

Credits:
Authors: Celia Stone, Elizabeth Franks, Myra Nicholson
Project Director: Sherrill B. Flora
Editors: Sherrill B. Flora, Karen Seberg
Special Education Consultants: Patricia Ann Seldon
Cover Design: Terri Moll
Inside Illustration: Valery Larson
Text Design: River Road Graphics

Standard Book Number: 1-56822-938-0
Reading Success—Book 6
Copyright © 2000 by LDA
a division of Instructional Fair Group
a Tribune Education Company
3195 Wilson Drive NW
Grand Rapids, Michigan 49544

Preface

If your child/student is struggling to read, write, and spell, this book will help you. It has been designed to be used by teachers, parents, or tutors who have no specialist training in the teaching of dyslexic children.

As co-authors, we are two teachers and a teacher/speech therapist who, after a long association with children with specific learning difficulties or dyslexia, decided to put together, in book form, a collection of our most interesting and successful teaching materials. We have gleaned ideas from many sources and built on them in a carefully constructed multisensory form, using a "seeing, saying, listening, writing" approach. *Reading Success* draws on the work of our predecessors in the field – Gillingham/Stillman/Orton, Hickey, Cowdrey, and others whose methods have become the foundation of this kind of teaching.

The program has been developed over a number of years and has been used successfully in its present form as the main scheme of work in the Dyslexia Units at Brontë House School, Bradford, at Clevedon House, Ilkley, and in the Speech and Language Unit at Fir Tree Middle School, Leeds, England. It has also been particularly successful with students having individual tutoring.

This is the sixth of a series of workbooks designed to take students progressively from the very first stages of letter recognition to full literacy. It is a **"reading through spelling"** program and ensures that the problems of spelling and writing are overcome as the child learns to read.

We realize that one of the problems is a short attention span and we have therefore made every effort to ensure that the exercises are as varied and entertaining as possible.

Table of Contents

How to Use This Book

Tutorial for all users, teachers, and parents

Materials Needed

Before you begin, make sure you have the following items ready to use with this book.

- **a set of wooden or plastic alphabet letters**
  both capital and lowercase
- **permanent marker pen**
  for drawing on Reading Pack cards
- **water-based marker pens**
  for writing spelling choices on Sound Picture/Spelling cards
- **sharp pencil**
- **tape recorder**
- **blank tape**
  student's practice tape
- **a set of crayons**
- **highlighter pen**
- **ruler**
- **scissors**
- **Reading and Spelling Pack Cards pages 215 to 224**
  Photocopy pages 215 to 224 from the book. Each student will need a set of cards.
- **an exercise book**
  Photocopy lined paper, page 36.

In addition to these materials, you may like to try using the following:

- **pencil grip**
- **egg timer or stopwatch**
- **dictionary**
- **thesaurus**
- **access to a word processor would be an advantage**

Introduction

Tutorial for all users, teachers, and parents

Reading Success Book 6 is very straightforward and easy to use. You will find all of the necessary instructions on the exercise pages. However, before you get started, we suggest you read through these guidelines to enable you to use the material more effectively.

This is the sixth and last book in this series and the material involves quite difficult learning processes for the student with specific learning difficulties. The style and presentation is geared to the slightly older student and to maintaining interest and attention. Visual presentation of cluewords through cartoons serves to make them memorable.

A full list of materials required for the exercises can be found on page 8. If you have worked through *Books 1, 2, 3, 4,* and *5* you will probably have most of the items.

If your student has not worked through *Books 1-5* in this series, the tests on pages 42–48 will help you to assess whether he/she is ready for *Book 6.* If these reveal any gaps in your student's phonic knowledge, it is vital to deal with them before starting on this book.

Material covered in *Books 1-5* includes:

Handwriting skills

Formation of capital and lowercase letters

Sequencing of the alphabet

Techniques of: "Read, Record, Listen, Repeat, Spell, Write"

    Working with Sound Pictures

    Working with word families and rhyming skills

Instant words

Identifying consonants and vowels and using these skills for splitting words into syllables—an essential skill to assist the decoding of longer and more difficult words

Essential spellings (These are spellings which do not fit into the structure but which are necessary for the student to know because of their frequency of occurrence in all reading material.)

Practicing two- and three-letter consonant blends

Introduction to nouns, verbs, adjectives, prepositions, contractions, the possessive pronoun "their," the past tense/suffix "ed," and use of a thesaurus

Telling the time

Learning more about prefixes and suffixes

Mind mapping

Long vowel sounds

It is often found that when children are really struggling with literacy it pays to begin at the beginning. When trying to slot students who already have some phonic skill into the system, it is frequently necessary to backtrack to ensure that all the links are established between the alphabetic name of the letter, the sound of the letter, recognition of the letter symbol, and the ability to write the letter neatly. If you consider that your student is not ready to start on this book after completing the pages 42 - 48, it is strongly recommended that you go back to the earlier books in the *Reading Success* series, all of which also contain assessment tests.

Lesson Guidelines

The daily lesson should consist of:

Marking the previous day's worksheets

Practicing the Reading Pack

Doing alphabet work where needed

Practicing the Spelling Pack and spelling words with alphabet letters if needed to reinforce work done

Completing the new sheets

Playing some reading games

Students should be praised and/or rewarded whenever they have made a real effort.

This section covers the various aspects of a typical lesson and also explains some of the exercises and how they should be tackled.

You will notice that every time a new letter pattern is introduced a similar format is followed.

1. Using the Alphabet Letters for Spelling

Book 4 introduced the concept of quartiles (a means of dividing the dictionary into manageable sections or quarters). Students were taught to place the alphabet letters in four rows:

A B C D (1st quartile) **E F G H I J K L M** (2nd quartile)

N O P Q R (3rd quartile) **S T U V W X Y Z** (4th quartile)

Help your student remember the first letter of every row by using the mnemonic "**A**ll **E**ggs **N**eed **S**alt."

Having completed five books, your student should now be gaining confidence, increasing his/her attention span, and improving his/her auditory memory. Alphabet exercises using the wooden letters in the above format are useful to review any spelling sounds with which your student is having difficulty. You may also use wooden letters in quartiles to review spellings or practice new spelling patterns. Have your student choose letters from the quartiles to spell a given word. These are then replaced before you move on to the next word. This repetition helps your student become familiar with the sequencing of the alphabet. Finally, call a sequence of letters at random. Have your student repeat the sequence as he/she puts the letters away. Your student should now be able to cope with a sequence of five letters. Competition helps here. If your student gets the sequence of letters correct, he/she gains a point. If not, you gain a point.

Spelling choices should be practiced to emphasize the fact that sounds can often be spelled in more than one way. Later in the lesson, dictate these words to your student to see if there is retention of what has been taught. If not retained by the student, the words need to be drilled again the following day.

Remember that this is a structured course. Words for spelling must contain only the letters already covered at any stage. For example, the **oy** sound may be used only when the student has progressed to pages 57–60 or beyond.

The alphabet is a considerable hurdle on the route to literacy and has to be something with which your student is able to confidently cope.

2. Auditory and Visual Introductions

For best learning results students must become active learners. When a new letter or concept is first introduced it is vital to have your student's full attention. I think one gets the best results when new introductions are made with direct instruction and some active discovery on the student's part. The introductions should also be somewhat consistent. This population of learners feels more secure when there is some consistency. When a new letter or concept is first introduced, there needs to be much teacher/tutor involvement.

Procedure: **Auditory Introduction**
Student needs to be reminded to: Listen, Repeat, Discover, and Answer

Say, "I will give you a list of words; you need to listen carefully to each word. Repeat each word after me. Try to discover what sounds are alike in each word: bat, bid, band, sob, tab."

Say, "What sound was the same in each of these words?" If the student is not able to answer, then repeat the process. This time accent the letter/sound you are trying to introduce.

Procedure: **Visual Introduction**
Student needs to be reminded to: Listen and Watch carefully

Write the words on the board. These are the same words used for the auditory introduction. Say each sound as you write the corresponding letter. Make sure you have your student's attention.

Ask your student to watch as you point to each letter and sound out the word.

Ask your student what letter or letters make the sound you just introduced in the auditory introduction.

Word List for Auditory and Visual Introductions

1. **ur** `e r`
   hurt turn church burp

2. **oy** `o y`
   toy joy boy soy

3. **oi** `o y`
   soil void coin moist

4. **ie** `E`
   chief yield priest pier

5. **ie** `I`
   pie lie die vie

6. **au** `a w`
   fault haul taut sauce

7. **ph** `f`
   photo phone phase graph

8. **ew** `U`
   stew crew new few

9. **aw** `a w`
   paw claw saw jaw

10. **-sion** `s h' n`
    mansion tension passion pension

11. **-sion** `z h' n`
    division television version

12. **ue** `OO`
    glue true clue blue

13. **-ous** `U s`
    famous jealous nervous

14. **ch** `k`
    school chord orchid echo

15. **ch** `s h`
    chef machine chute brochure

16. **or** `ə r` **or** in an unaccented syllable
    horror doctor tutor actor

17. **wor** `w ə r` **or** after the letter **w**
    worm work world word

18. **ou** `OO`
    soup youth wound group

19. **ou** `U`
    touch young couple trouble

20. **eigh** `A`
    eight sleigh neighbor

21. **ei** `A`
    vein skein veil

22. **ei** `E`
    ceiling conceit receive

23. **ey** `E`
    donkey kidney monkey

24. **ey** `A`
    prey they obey

25. **ar** `ə r` **ar** in an unaccented syllable
    dollar collar burglar

26. **eu** `U`
    feud Europe neutral

27. **ui** `U`
    fruit suit juice bruise

28. **oe** `O`
    toe Joe woe

3. Listen to the Teacher Section

Simply read the words, steadily and clearly to the student, giving him/her plenty of time to consider whether the sound listened for has been heard.

Transcript for the Auditory Exercises Which Accompany *Book 6*

The teacher reads this section of the lesson to the child. For independent students, the teacher may wish to tape record this section for the student.

Page 43, Section 1: SPELLING TEST
    1. athlete 2. remained 3. highlight 4. headline 5. motherland 6. snowbound
    7. feeble 8. beautiful 9. centigrade 10. cycle 11. recent 12. overture
    13. gentlemen 14. loud 15. gin 16. knowing 17. gracefully 18. boatyard
    19. flirting 20. matchbox

Page 49, Section 6: Write **ur** in the box if you hear ⬛**e r**⬛ in the word.
    1. burning 2. surfers 3. garden 4. storing 5. urgent 6. curly 7. spartan
    8. unfurling

Page 54, Section 4: SPELLING TEST
    1. purpose 2. service 3. shirt 4. surplus 5. circle 6. merger 7. surface
    8. swirling 9. nerve 10. certify

Page 57, Section 6: Write **oy** in the box if you hear ⬛**o y**⬛ at the end of the word.
    1. coy 2. toy 3. spray 4. Troy 5. crow 6. convoy 7. alloy 8. how
    9. destroy 10. joy

Page 65, Section 6: Write **oi** in the box if you hear ⬛**o y**⬛ in the word.
    1. toil 2. choice 3. place 4. avoid 5. house 6. poison 7. exploit 8. join
    9. horse 10. noise

Page 71, Section 6: Write **ie** in the box if you hear ⬛**E**⬛ in the word.
    1. field 2. chief 3. storm 4. diesel 5. vane 6. grieve 7. brief 8. barn

Page 77, Section 6: Write **ie** in the box if you hear ⬛**I**⬛ at the end of the word.
    1. pie 2. pray 3. sea 4. fie 5. tune 6. die 7. tie 8. lie

Page 82, Section 5: Write each word as an abbreviation in your exercise book.
    1. Professor 2. Thursday 3. square 4. centimeter 5. October 6. Captain
    7. United Nations 8. kilogram 9. Doctor 10. post meridiem

Page 83, Section 6: Write **au** in the box if you hear [aw] in the word.
    I. sauce 2. applause 3. ouch 4. cause 5. gauze 6. paunch 7. case 8. ounce

Page 86, Section 1: Listen carefully. In each line, underline or highlight the word you hear.
    I. sauce 2. flaunt 3. launder 4. automatic 5. haunt

Page 86, Section 2: Listen to each word. Write the word under **ou** [ow] or **au** [aw].
    I. proud 2. pause 3. pouch 4. paunch 5. hound 6. mouse 7. haunt 8. bouncing
    9. caution 10. automatic

Page 90, Section 6: Write **ph** in the box if you hear [f] in the word.
    I. phone 2. elephant 3. dolphin 4. graph 5. moth 6. orphan 7. shut 8. gopher

Page 92, Section 2: Write the words you hear under correct headings.
   1. cuff   2. graph   3. stuff   4. fan   5. phrase   6. tough   7. fox   8. cough

Page 98, Section 6: Write **ew** in the box if you hear **U** or **oo** in the word.
   1. stew   2. pewter   3. nephew   4. niece   5. mildew   6. uncle   7. chew   8. jewel

Page 99, Section 5: Write the headings "st**ew** **U**" and "cr**ew** **oo**" in your exercise book. Listen carefully and write each word in the correct column.
   1. shrew   2. new   3. chew   4. few   5. stew   6. flew   7. drew   8. view   9. grew

Page 104, Section 2: Write the answers to these questions in your exercise book.
   1. What is the name of an angle which is less than 180 but more than 90 degrees?
   2. What is the name of a straight line drawn through the center of a circle?
   3. What is another name for an angle of 90 degrees?
   4. What is the name of the longest side of a triangle?
   5. What is the name of the perimeter of a circle?
   6. A number made by multiplying another number by itself, for example 2 x 2, is called what?
   7. The number below the line in a fraction is called what?
   8. A mathematical statement that 2 things are equal is called what?
   9. The distance from the center of a circle to the circumference is called what?
   10. The extent of a surface is the what?

Page 104, Section 3: Solve the riddle by answering each question "Yes" or "No" and writing the appropriate letter in the box.
   1. Is the perimeter of a square called the circumference? Yes or no?
   2. Is a triangle with 2 equal sides and 2 equal angles called an isosceles triangle?
   3. Is an equation a mathematical statement that 2 things are equal?
   4. Is the number above the line in a fraction called the denominator?
   5. Is a ratio a diagram of the relationship between two variables?
   6. Is a unit for measuring angles called a degree?
(The answer is RADIUS)

Page 105, Section 6: Write **aw** in the box if you hear **aw** in the word.
   1. claw   2. thaw   3. sprawl   4. crawl   5. crow   6. squawk   7. awful   8. sprain

Page 106, Section 1: Check the word you hear.
   1. cow   2. saw   3. drawn   4. raw   5. owning   6. bawl   7. down   8. awe
   9. low   10. brawn

Page 108, Section 2: Listen carefully to this story about relatives. Answer the questions.

Hello. My name is Bridget. I have a brother who is 4 years younger than I and a sister who is 2 years older. My sister is married and has moved away from home. She has twin daughters who are 11 months old. When they learn to talk they will call me Auntie. My little brother in an uncle. My sister's husband is called Joe and he is now my brother-in-law. He is 25 and one year older than my sister.

How old am I and how old are my sister and brother?

My mother is now a delighted grandmother. She loves children and would have liked to have had even more of her own, but she was 40 when my brother was born. We are all much younger than our cousins because my aunt, who is 5 years older than my mother, had her first child when she was only 20.

How old is my mother and how old is my aunt and her first child?

(Answers: Bridget is 22 years old. Her sister is 24 and her brother is 18. Bridget's mother is 58 and her aunt is 63. The aunt's first child is now 43 years old.)

Page 109, Section 2: Write each word in the correct column.
1. energy 2. graceful 3. curl 4. foolish 5. anger 6. noisy 7. fool 8. angry
9. curly 10. grace 11. noise 12. energetic

Page 110, Section 1: Listen and fill in the blanks to complete the sentences.
1. He insists he saw a flying saucer last Thursday night.
2. The Japanese love raw squid dipped in horseradish sauce.
3. No one knows what caused dinosaurs to become extinct.
4. The exhaust coming from Paul's car is against the law.
5. The author attended the launch of his latest book and agreed to sign copies of the first edition for the audience.
6. I love pawpaw but I have never tasted mango or strawberries.
7. The children caught the trout when fishing in the river.
8. Jaundice is a disease of the liver and causes yellowing of the skin.
9. Laura went to audition for a part in the pantomime.
10. A lovely turquoise shawl covered her scrawny shoulders.

Page 110, Section 2: SPELLING TEST

    1. turning 2. squirted 3. service 4. annoy 5. children 6. onion 7. tomatoes
    8. spoiled 9. grief 10. diesel 11. loaves 12. untie 13. pause 14. typhoon
    5. although 16. few 17. grew 18. strawberry 19. diameter 20. Italy

Page 115, Section 1: Write each word you hear in the correct column.

    1. permission 2. caption 3. expansion 4. caution 5. option 6. addiction
    7. affection 8. recession 9. admission 10. expulsion

Page 118, Section 6: Write **ue** in the box if you hear **u** or **oo** at the end of the word.

    1. glue 2. rescue 3. continue 4. collect 5. flowers 6. virtue 7. pursue 8. locate

Page 123, Section 1: Listen carefully and add the correct words to these sentences.

    1. We went wrong because we did not follow all the signs as we went on a walk.
    2. The folk festival was a great success. The weather was mild and balmy so that
        we did not need to wrap up to keep warm.
    3. The knight's knees were knocking loudly as he squared up to his opponent at the
        jousting contest. They clashed so violently, they had to be wrenched apart.
    4. I felt numb as we knelt down and unwrapped the limbs of the embalmed
        mummy in the tomb.

Page 124, Section 6: Write **ous** in the box if you hear **U s** in the word.

    1. jealous 2. humorous 3. instantaneous 4. mistaken 5. irritation 6. simultaneous
    7. famous 8. marvelous

Page 125, Section 1: Listen carefully. Write a number 1 in the box of the first word you hear, a number 2 in the box of the second and so on.

    1. famous 2. jealous 3. treacherous 4. ridiculous 5. marvelous 6. tremendous
    7. generous 8. venomous 9. poisonous 10. adventurous

Page 127, Section 3: Write the words you hear next to the correct headings.

    1. hideous 2. nervous 3. bonus 4. octopus 5. contemptuous 6. simultaneous
    7. pompous 8. sumptuous

Page 128, Section 6: Write **ch** in the box if you hear **k** in the word.

    1. ache 2. chrome 3. monarch 4. honor 5. match 6. character 7. absorption
    8. scheme 9. chaos 10. echo

Page 131, Section 6: Write **ch** in the box if you hear **s h** in the word.

    1. chef 2. machine 3. brochure 4. moustache 5. bravery 6. unsuitably
    7. parachute 8. chiffon 9. choice 10. chivalry

Page 132, Section 3: Write each word you hear in the correct column.
I. Christmas 2. choir 3. Charlotte 4. checking 5. school 6. chalets 7. choosing
8. challenge 9. brochure

Page 143, Section 2: Listen carefully to this story. How much can you remember?
The Sun (which is not a planet) is getting hotter and hotter and a thermometer explodes
and breaks so that Mercury rolls out in balls. The goddess Venus picks them up and
takes them to Earth. She asks a man who is eating a Mars bar to bury them. He says
his name is Jupiter and he is wearing a black leather jacket with a picture of the Sun
on the back. He tells her that the letters S-U-N stand for Saturn, Uranus, and Neptune.
Just then his little dog Pluto runs up to join them.

Page 150, Section 3: Listen to these words and write each word in the correct column.
I. pearl 2. care 3. fear 4. search 5. beard 6. wear 7. learn 8. swear 9. gears
I0. earn II. yearn 12. heard 13. earth 14. dearth 15. early 16. tear 17. bear
18. pear 19. scare 20. hair 21. there 22. rear 23. dear 24. hearing. 25. near
26. spear 27. clear

Page 152, Section 4: SPELLING TEST
I. procession 2. division 3. argue 4. wrong 5. fabulous 6. monarch
7. avalanche 8. optician 9. medal 10. earn II. wear 12. conscience
13. experience 14. familiar 15. lawyer 16. recognize 17. argument 18. official
19. restaurant 20. knickers

Page 160, Section 6: Write **or** in the box if you hear **ə r** in the word.
I. advisor 2. harmful 3. calculator 4. bachelor 5. actor 6. doctor 7. awnings
8. sponsor 9. microphone 10. mirror

Page 161, Section 4: Underline the stressed syllable in each word.
I. thirty 2. turnip 3. injection 4. calculator 5. senator 6. adventurer
7. malnutrition

Page 169, Section 2: Listen for an example of onomatopoeia in this poem by Robert Louis
Stevenson.
From a Railway carriage Faster than fairies, faster than witches Bridges and houses,
hedges and ditches; And charging along like troops in a battle, All through the mead-
ows the horses and cattle: All of the sights of the hill and the plain Fly as thick as driving rain; And ever again, in the wink of an eye, Painted stations whistle by. Here is a
child who clambers and scrambles, All by himself and gathering brambles; Here is a
tramp who stands and gazes; And there is the green for stringing the daisies! Here is
a cart run away in the road Lumping along with man and load; And here is a mill, and
there is a river: Each a glimpse and gone forever!

Page 173, Section 2: Write the words you hear in the correct columns.
1. cousin 2. young 3. wound 4. double 5. soup 6. youth 7. group 8. country
9. couple 10. uncouth 11. trouble 12. croup

Page 175, Section 2: Listen carefully. Write a number 1 in the box of the first word you hear, a number 2 in the box of the second and so on.
1. ate (consumed) 2. vein (blood vessel) 3. vale (valley) 4. reigns (rules) 5. their (possessing) 6. veil (cover) 7. way (path) 8. typhoon 9. weigh (to measure) 10. vane (shows wind direction) 11. slay (kill) 12. eight (number) 13. Dane (from Denmark) 14. deign (consent) 15. weight (heaviness) 16. wait (delay) 17. sleigh (vehicle with runners) 18. reins (guide a horse) 19. there (place) 20. rains (precipitation) 21. vain (conceited)

Page 180, Section 1: Write each word in the correct column.
1. cheerful 2. please 3. athlete 4. chiefly 5. protein 6. hygiene 7. completely
8. receipt 9. sweeping 10. grease

Worksheet 80, Section 2:
1. It is difficult to believe that he has lost so much weight.
2. The conceited woman ignored his remarks about her foreign accent.
3. The chief of police introduced electronic surveillance techniques in order to seize the thief.
4. He received a small fortune for the masterpiece which was auctioned to a wealthy sheik.
5. Despite fierce competition, he achieved first place.
6. His niece picked up the receiver when the phone rang.

Page 184, Section 6: Write **ar** in the box if you hear ⟨ə r⟩ in the word.
1. dollar 2. collar 3. cellar 4. corn 5. grammar 6. available 7. amount
8. perpendicular

Page 185, Section 2: Number the words as you hear them.
1. perpendicular 2. activator 3. blackmailer 4. adviser 5. subscriber
6. aggressor 7. bullfighter 8. professor 9. mortar 10. chronometer
11. grammar 12. dictator 13. alligator 14. beggar 15. molecular

Page 190, Section 3: Fill in the blanks to complete the story. The words in Sections 1 and 2 will help you.

Eunice and Eustace met on a cruise aboard the S.S. Eureka. Eustace first noticed Eunice during a competition when he made a fool of himself to gain her attention and accidentally stood on her foot. This resulted in a painful bruise on her big toe.

He tried to pour oil on troubled water by bringing her a fruit cocktail made of sloes and lime and lemon juice while apologizing profusely. Unfortunately, the bruise caused inflammation and swelling which masked a serious condition, subsequently diagnosed by a neurologist. Eunice filed a suit to sue Eustace who was sadly unable to appear in court as he was suffering from pneumonia. Eunice was full of woe when she heard of Eustace's serious condition and the suit was dropped. She visited him daily, doing many helpful tasks like hoeing his garden. She took her oboe and played peaceful music to try to help him to relax and recover.

Page 207, Section 1:

The Reader's Digest Great Illustrated Dictionary describes the etymology of English metaphorically, as a river, like this: The English language is like a river—a mighty Amazon among rivers, springing up from many sources and drawing nourishment from many tributaries. By the 8th century the main stream could be discerned in the old English spoken by Anglo-Saxons. When we speak of man, woman, and child, of bread and meat we are using their tongue. The powerful tributary that came from France after the Norman Conquest gave us male, female, infant, and a host of other words including crust and beef. Latin, old Norse, German, Arabic, and many other languages all added their contributions. Downstream the river broadened as it was joined by tributaries carrying the languages of science, technology, economics, sport, and other specialized areas of life. In recent years these streams have contributed words and phrases such as quasar and quango, black hole and biodegradable, hang gliding and hardwired. As the river flowed on, it branched into a delta, with channels carrying the varieties of Australia, New Zealand, India, South Africa, the Caribbean, Canada, the U.S.A. and others along with the mother tongue down to the sea of Word English.

4. Reading Pack

Figure 1

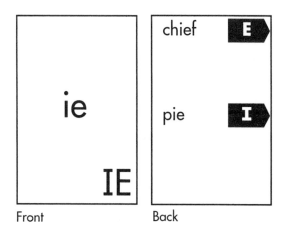

Front   Back

It is vital that the student practices the Reading Pack regularly, preferably daily. He/she will be adding to this LOOKING and SAYING Pack through page 189 of this book.

1) First the student must LOOK at the letters on the front.

2) Without turning the card over, he/she tries to remember and SAY the clueword and its sound; for example, chief **E**. If the student is unable to recall the clueword, he/she turns the card over, looks at the picture, says the clueword and sound, and then puts the card at the bottom of the pack.

3) If the clueword is remembered, the student turns the card over and checks that what he/she said is correct.

4) If correct, start the stack of correct cards by placing the card, letter side down, picture side up, on the table and then proceed to the next card. If not correct, put the card at the back of the pack to come up again at the end of the sequence.

Using a stopwatch to record the time your student takes to progress through the pack can be motivating; he/she can try to beat his/her own record.

5. Sound Picture/Spelling Pack

Figure 2

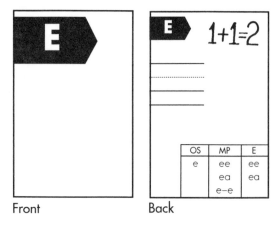

Front   Back

This is the HEARING and WRITING Pack.

On the FRONT of the card is the Sound Picture, which is one or more white letters in a black pentagon. It is a symbol representing the sound to be said instead of the letter's name. It is designed to aid orientation and indicates the left to right direction needed for reading and spelling. (See Figure 2.)

For example, this is the Sound Picture for the long vowel **E**.

Contrast this with the Sound Picture for the short vowel **e**.

On the BACK of the card is the information that the student needs to complete the associations relevant to that particular sound.

TOP LEFT—The Sound Picture (see Figure 2 on previous page)

Immediately below this you will see the blank handwriting format. This enables the teacher to write the relevant form of the letter (upper- or lowercase), or the spelling choice, where more than one exists (for example, **e, ee, ea, e-e,** or **ie**). This is designed to reinforce the concept of choice in the spelling of sounds. Refer to the example for Sound Picture exercises in Figures 3 and 4 on page 25. If the cards have been laminated the relevant spelling choice should be written on the handwriting format using a water-based felt pen. This can then be wiped off and changed as necessary. If laminated cards are not used then new cards can be issued at any time and changed as needed.

TOP RIGHT—The Clueword Picture

Below this is an example of the handwritten form of the letter/s on handwriting format with the second or third spelling choice where applicable.

BOTTOM RIGHT—Only applicable to long vowel sounds when a miniature of the Long Vowel Choices Chart is shown. Until pages 71–74, the LVCC will look like Figure 2, but after page 74 has been completed an extra spelling choice (chief **E**) will need to be added.

To use the Sound Picture/Spelling Pack, tell the student, "This is your HEARING and WRITING Pack. It tells you which sound to listen for with your ears (the front of the card) and how to write it correctly (the back of the card)."

1) The teacher says the sound, for example **E**, and the student responds by repeating the sound **E** and then naming the letters **e, ee, ea,** and **e-e**. In this example these letters would be written on the Long Vowel Choices Chart. The student must say "Open syllable **E** spelled **e.** Main part of the word—1st Choice—spelled **ee**, 2nd Choice spelled **ea**, 3rd Choice **e-e**, and (only after page 74 has been completed), 4th Choice **ie**." The student may then fill them in on the Long Vowel Choices Chart. (See pages 225 and 226.)

When working alone, the student must have the front of the Sound Picture card facing him/her, for example, **E**. While looking at this the student must say the sound **E** and then continue as above.

2) In the case of other letter patterns, for example short vowels or consonants, the letter/s must be written on a copy of the lined practice sheet.

3) When the letter has been written, the student turns over the card and compares his/her handwriting with the example. If it is incorrect, it goes to the bottom of the pack for a second try, as with the Reading Pack. At first you may need to practice this routine with your student, but eventually he/she should be able to do this task independently. It will be necessary to check from time to time that this is being done properly.

6. The Long Vowel Choices Chart

The Long Vowel Choices Chart (found on pages 225 and 226.) provides a systematic way of recording the various long vowel spelling patterns. The student is taught to write these spelling choices in different columns according to their position in words and most likely usage. Choices are introduced one at a time and the student revises the chart when practicing the Spelling Pack Cards. The Long Vowel Choices Chart becomes a reference sheet and an aid to checking spelling using a dictionary. The most likely choice is marked "1st try." The student must look up the word using the spelling listed under "1st try." If not found, he/she should move systematically through the other possible choices until the correct spelling is found.

To help the student to master the Long Vowel Choices Chart there is a system whereby spelling choices are recorded as puzzle pieces which the student identifies and then builds into a visual framework and memory aid. For example, in Section 3 on page 74, the student is instructed to find the puzzle piece on page 74 matching the one illustrated on the worksheet, cut it out, and place it on the Long Vowel Choices Chart. Further puzzle pieces will be accumulated as more long vowel choices are introduced. Completing the puzzle daily, using the self-checking facility on the back of each Spelling Pack card, will help to reinforce the concept of where the long vowel sound appears in the word. Be sure to help your student to make the link between the Long Vowel Choices Chart and the Spelling Pack and to connect these strategies to their applications in all written work.

7. The Sound Picture/Spelling Pack and
Sound Pictures → Word Exercises

By the time students have reached this final book in the series, they should be able to complete pages 111 and 170, without the concrete use of the actual sound pictures. However, if they find this difficult they may continue to make the words from the Sound Picture/Spelling Pack together with the necessary consonants from previous books, filling in the correct spelling choices, and then turning over and overlapping the sounds to spell the word.

Sometimes a Sound Picture is different from the letter that you write. For example, the Sound Picture **s** can be written as **s** or **ss**. The **c** spelling of the **s** sound before letters **y**, **i**, and **e** is introduced on page 97 of *Book 4* and the **ce** spelling of the **s** sound is introduced on page 99. Therefore from page 100 of *Book 4* on, response to the Sound Picture **s** will be:

s ss cy ci ce

Similarly the response to the sound picture **j** can be written as:

j   ge   dge

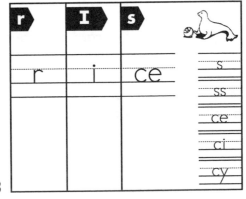

Figure 3   Figure 4

The student selects the spelling choice required and writes it under the Sound Picture, using a water-based pen.

This logo reminds the student that it is time to practice the Reading and Sound Picture/Spelling Pack.

8. Instant Words/Essential Spellings

These words have been discontinued in this book. We suggest that instead you use the blank spelling program on page 38 as an individual program for your students, concentrating on the spelling patterns which they find difficult. Remember to cluster spelling patterns together for reinforcement, for example add, adding, addition, additive, addiction; caught, taught, naught; and bought, thought, sought.

Pages 141–142 and page 208 feature words which are commonly misspelled.

9. Reading Games for Instant Words
(and other difficult words)

Write each word on four cards so that a group of 10 words = a pack of 40 cards. These cards can then be used for traditional games of SNAP, RUMMY, PELMANISM (PAIRS), HAPPY FAMILIES, or simply for sorting. The word should be read silently every time it is picked up. The cards may also be used with board games, or any game involving the throwing of dice.

Family Fours

This game is played with a minimum of three players. Cards are placed facedown in the middle of the table and each player in turn picks up a card and reads it. The card is then placed faceup in front of the player.

The next player reads his/her card and checks whether there are any matching cards, or having the same letter pattern, in front of any other player. If he/she spots one, he/she is entitled to ask the player for this card (or cards) which is then placed in his/her family collection on the table. In this way a complete "family" of any four cards is built up. The winner is the player who collects the most families. See page 80 of *Book 4* and page 147 of *Book 5*.

Blackboard Bingo

The teacher writes a list of words (at least 15) on the board or on a sheet of paper. Each student chooses five or six of these words from the list and writes them down. The teacher then reads aloud from the list on the board at random. Students cross words off their lists as they are read. The first student to cross out all the words on his/her list shouts "Bingo" and is the winner.

More fun activities for alphabet work and for using with Reading Pack and Sound Picture/Spelling Pack are covered in Section 1 and Section 5 of this tutorial.

Don't forget the value of mnemonics for teaching spelling patterns. For example to teach the irregular spelling pattern for could/would/should, try telling your student to say "O U Lucky Duck." To teach the word "because" say "Big Elephants Can't Always Use Small Exits." Some more of these are demonstrated on pages 64 and 100 of *Book 5*. Your students will have fun making up their own mnemonics for difficult spelling patterns.

10. Syllable Splitting

Students were introduced to **vc** patterning and splitting in *Books 1, 2, 3, 4,* and *5*. They learned Rule 1, the most common way to split **vc/cv** (for example, rab/bit) words and Rule 2, the most common way to split **v/cv** (for example, ro/bot) words. *Book 4* introduced Rule 3, the less common **vc/v** pattern (for example, rob/in) words. When working with unfamiliar **vcv** words students will need to experiment, trying first Rule 2 and then Rule 3 to see which one sounds correct. Example: ca/bin (✗) or cab/in (✓). See page 55 of *Book 5* and page 120 of this book where students are expected to apply these principles to the reading of longer words. Students should pattern from the first vowel to the last vowel and then apply the above rules.

Example: **vc / cvc / cvc / cv**
             e s / t a b / l i<u>sh</u> / ment

Remember that consonant, digraphs, for example, **wh**, **sh**, **ch**, are treated as one sound.

11. Controlled Vocabulary

Reading and Spelling passages throughout the series are carefully structured to contain only letters that have been taught. Students are never asked to read or write (with the exception of Instant Words/Essential Spellings) words whose patterns have not been covered in the structure. This builds confidence and a feeling of success.

12. Word Families and Rhyming

Remember that limericks, jokes, and humorous verse are valuable aids in the teaching of reading and comprehension. Make these kinds of materials available to your students. You may need to teach them to understand, as well as to read, the jokes.

13. Grammar

Basic elements of grammar have been introduced throughout the series. See the Table of Contents pages of each book to find work on specific rules.

14. Irlen Syndrome
(Scotopic Sensitivity Syndrome)

Many children have difficulty with black print on white paper. We suggest that teachers experiment using various pastel shades of paper when photocopying. This will establish which color is most helpful in reducing the glare and distortion which may be experienced by children suffering from Irlen Syndrome or Scotopic Sensitivity Syndrome.

If the student is helped by the colored paper, try using colored overlays on top of reading material.

We hope that by the end of *Book 6* your students have gained confidence and are feeling positive about their ability to read, write, and spell at an advanced level. Well done!

15. Letter Record Page

This logo represents the Record Page found on page 29. When the student has worked satisfactorily on new sounds as they are introduced (for example, nurse **e r** on page 49–53) and completed this section satisfactorily, he/she simply finds the section on the Record Page with the **ur** spelling pattern. The student may either color in the section or check it off. By the time *Book 6* has been completed, the Record Page should also be complete. Note that where there are two or more spellings of the same sound, a Sound Picture is given.

Make sure your student knows the sound, name, and written shape o f the letters and the appropriate spelling choice rule before allowing him/her to fill in the record.

Record page

-ge
gi
gy

-cian

o-e

oe

ce
ci
cy

-tion

e-e

-sion

-ice

ar

ee

-dge

us

wh

i-e

ie

ow

a-e

oo

oa

au ea ou

us ai aw

eu ir

-y ui

er ew

oy or

ch ay

ei ur

u-e -ue

oi ph

-le ey

-ic	-ture	igh
-age	ear	-our
-tch	or	ous

16. Notes to the worksheets

In this, the final book of the series, the vocabulary is becoming more difficult. You need to ensure that your students look up unknown words in the dictionary. They should now be getting more adept at dictionary skills (see pages 42, 59, 91, 102, 120, and 207), but you need to check from time to time that they are using the dictionary skills already taught and not reverting back to merely leafing through the dictionary. Draw your students' attention to the guide words at the top of each page.

In this book your student will be coming to terms with different ways of spelling the same sound. Have your student sort packets of words, which have only the vowel sound picture, into different spelling patterns. Check the groups of cards before the words are written to ensure that your student is not reinforcing incorrect spelling.

Example: **kw** **E** **n**
 dr **E** **m**
 th **E** **f**

Page 42, Section 1:

Ask your student, when the sentence has been written, to track the alphabet (putting a line through the first letter "a" found, then letter "b" and so on) to discover how many letters have been used more than once. You will then be able to observe his/her ability to sequence the alphabet. You may need to do more follow up work if your student finds this task difficult.

Page 43, Section 1:

Please note that this is a test. Do not prompt your student. Use the Record Sheet on page 39. By putting your student's reading deviations in the space below the spelling test, you will have a clearer understanding of his/her difficulties. It will be immediately obvious if you need to review the sounds and spellings taught in *Book 5* or earlier.

Section 2 on page 43 will also highlight any spelling patterns which need further review, before starting this book. Examples of words are on the following page.

Examples:

panic	adventure	head	scream	athlete	tonic	vulture
dead	stream	Pete	supersonic	scripture	bread	squeal
complete	Atlantic	denture	spread	appeal	discrete	frantic
capture	dreaded	gleam	deplete	scenic	departure	weather
repeat	concrete	chronic	nurture	peasant	creature	trapeze

glove	dazzle	ankle	uncle	tough	love	guzzle
fickle	miracle	ought	dove	puzzle	sparkle	article
enough	shove	drizzle	crackle	particle	trough	shovel
grizzle	pickle	vehicle	cough	wonder	muzzle	trickle
ventricle	bought	wonderful	frazzle	tinkle	barnacle	thought

Pages 52–53:

The story has been deliberately left open-ended so that the student may continue the story as requested in Section 2, picking up either of the strands, for example, the party in Hurst Castle or the novel being written by Lord Burton.

Pages 75–76:

To proofread successfully, teach your student to work from the end to the beginning, reading one word at a time. This mitigates against reading what you think it says!

Any spelling mistakes not discovered could be practiced on the blank spelling program sheet on page 38.

"After breakfast, we packed our bags and went to our next destination which was two miles away. Our Cub leader said it would take us one hour to get there, but we thought it would take longer and we set off. It did only take one hour.

When we got there, we pitched our tents. We pitched our tents quickly so we had time to go for a walk, which we did not like, but we made a deal that if we went for a walk, we could have a campfire that night. The walk was not too long and we got our badges for walking two miles and at least we had someone to talk to. It was nearly two o'clock so we had some lunch. We did do some archery and athletics, closely supervised, until five o'clock.

We had a bit of a shock at five o'clock because a sponsored walk came right through where our tents were pitched, so we had to move our tents. By the time we had moved our tents, it was getting dark and we had a campfire and the Cub leader had some marshmallows. We cooked them on the bonfire. Then we had a game of football in the dark. We pretended to go to sleep. When the Cub leader had gone, we sneaked out and got up to some mischief. We got back into our tents an hour or so later, then we just talked for the rest of the night."

The piece of writing would make a good discussion point.

a) On the positive side, this is a good piece of writing which gives an interesting picture of life at the Cub camp.

b) Sentences are too long in some parts. How could these be split up?

c) Writer needs to be taught the difference between "our" and "are" and "to," "two," and "too."

d) There were no paragraphs.

e) The concept of past tense verbs ending with "ed" needs to be taught.

f) Of which Spelling Pack sounds does the author need to be aware?

Page 110:
Where spelling choices are given you should make sure your student is familiar with many of the common words of each choice. More sorting activities should be done if your student is confused.

Page 111:
If your student finds this exercise difficult, revert to matching the Sound Pictures with the words listed, turning the cards over, and checking on pages 90 and 130 of *Book 5* using Spelling Pack Cards from previous books where necessary.

Page 132:
Sorting activities may also be necessary here.

Page 150:
Again, sorting activities may be necessary.

Games

Even at this stage games should be included as a valuable teaching tool. See pages 26 and 27.

Duff Definitions card game

Find the card sheets on pages 34 and 35. Photocopy the pages so that the cards line up correctly, back-to-back. Cut them out.

The words on these cards are homophones. Students often confuse their meanings.

Place the pack of cards, definition side down in the center of the table.

Play as "call my bluff!" Player 1 picks up a card, reads the word and one of the two meanings given. This may be the correct (bold type) or incorrect (regular type) meaning. Player 2 must decide which meaning was read. If Player 2 is correct, he/she takes the card and places it on the table in front of him/her to begin the pile of cards he/she has won. If he/she is incorrect, the next player suggests the correct definition and tries to win the card and so on.

Player 2 then picks up a card and tries to outwit Player 3 and so on.

The winner is the one with the most cards in his/her pile.

Spelling Assignment Sheet (Page 38):

Write in which words need to be practiced by your student, remembering to group words into patterns where possible. Your student should practice the words daily. Check his/her work; he/she may stop when five words have been spelled incorrectly. On the days following, continue to place checkmarks on the grid, until the student achieves 100% accuracy. You may stop testing for a word when the student spells it correctly for three consecutive days. Retest the word in ten days to see if the student has retained his/her ability to spell the word correctly.

Duff definitions

Words which sound the same or similar but have different meanings.
(For instructions, see page 33 of Teacher's Notes)

6 heir **the next in line (usually royal)** the stuff we breathe	**5** air **the stuff we breathe** the next in line (usually royal)	**4** excess a way in **more than enough**	**3** access more than enough **a way in**	**2** except **not including** to say "yes" to an invitation	**1** accept **to say "yes" to an invitation** not including
12 anti **against** adjoining (next to)	**11** ante **adjoining (next to)** against	**10** alter the holy table in a place of worship **to change something**	**9** altar to change something **the holy table in a place of worship**	**8** aloud **opposite of silently** permitted	**7** allowed **permitted** opposite of silently
18 birth **when one is born** a bunk on a ship	**17** berth **a bunk on a ship** when one is born	**16** beach **at the seaside** a type of tree	**15** beech **a type of tree** at the seaside	**14** bear without covering or clothes **a big, brown furry, animal**	**13** bare a big, brown, furry animal **without covering or clothes**
24 bored **uninterested** a thin flat piece of wood	**23** board **a thin flat piece of wood** uninterested	**22** boulder more confident **a large stone**	**21** bolder a large stone **more confident**	**20** blue **the color of a clear sky** past tense of to blow	**19** blew **past tense of to blow** the color of a clear sky
30 brakes **means of stopping** intervals or rests	**29** breaks **intervals or rests** means of stopping	**28** bury **to inter in the ground or grave** grows on bush (a fruit)	**27** berry **grows on bush (a fruit)** to inter in the ground or grave	**26** bow branch of tree **lower one's head in prayer or deference**	**25** bough lower one's head in prayer or deference **branch of tree**
36 cheque **a promise to pay via the bank** to examine or investigate (in Canada and England)	**35** check **to examine or investigate** a promise to pay via the bank	**34** serial **novel or play presented in installments** eaten for breakfast	**33** cereal **eaten for breakfast** novel or play presented in installments	**32** seller a cool dark basement **one with goods to sell**	**31** cellar one with goods to sell **a cool dark basement**

Duff definitions

Words which sound the same or similar but have different meanings.
(For instructions, see page 33.)

1 accept	2 except	3 access	4 excess	5 air	6 heir
7 allowed	**8** aloud	**9** altar	**10** alter	**11** ante	**12** anti
13 bare	**14** bear	**15** beech	**16** beach	**17** berth	**18** birth
19 blew	**20** blue	**21** bolder	**22** boulder	**23** board	**24** bored
25 bough	**26** bow	**27** berry	**28** bury	**29** breaks	**30** brakes
31 cellar	**32** seller	**33** cereal	**34** serial	**35** check	**36** cheque
					(in Canada and England)

Exercise Book Paper

Self assessment check list

What have you learned? What do you need to review?
Grade yourself from 1 (lowest) to 10 (highest) on each of these skills.

Spelling

Sound letter relationships ☐
Books 1–3
Spelling patterns *Book 4* ☐
        Book 5 ☐
        Book 6 ☐
Essential/frequent spellings ☐
Adding suffixes to silent "e" word ☐
Adding suffixes and doubling ☐
Plurals ☐
Sequencing and spelling the ☐
days of the week
Sequencing and spelling the ☐
months of the year
Written numbers ☐
Finding words which rhyme ☐

Writing

The alphabet ☐
Neat handwriting ☐
Good sentence structure ☐
Writing a post card ☐
Writing a letter to a friend ☐
Writing a formal letter ☐
Essay planning ☐
Writing an imaginative story ☐
Writing from your own experience ☐
Writing a discussion ☐
Writing a summary ☐
Writing checks ☐
Filling in forms ☐
Writing an advertisement ☐

Punctuation

Correct use of capital letters ☐
Periods and question marks ☐
Contractions ☐
Apostrophes ☐

Reading

Recognizing open and closed syllables ☐
Recognizing short vowel sounds ☐
Recognizing long vowel sound patterns ☐
Reading 1 syllable words ☐
Reading 2 syllable words ☐
Reading 3 syllable words ☐
Reading 3++ syllable words ☐
Reading and following instructions ☐
Understanding a short piece of writing ☐
Understanding a more complex ☐
piece of writing
Noting key points, words, or sentences ☐
Reading aloud to other people ☐
Using a dictionary ☐
Using a thesaurus ☐
Understanding abbreviations ☐
Reading a timetable ☐
Math vocabulary ☐
Science vocabulary ☐

Grammar

Knowing what a noun is ☐
        verb ☐
        adjective ☐
        adverb ☐
        preposition ☐
        conjunction ☐

Other skills

Planning for homework ☐
Listening to instructions ☐
Telling the time ☐
24-hour clock ☐
Review planning ☐
Use of Mindmaps ☐

Spelling Assignment Record Page

(See page 33 for instructions.)

Name _____

Date _____

Date													
1													
2													
3													
4													
5													
6													
7													
8													
9													
10													
11													
12													
13													
14													
15													
16													
17													
18													
19													
20													
21													
22													
Total													

Record Sheet for Responses to Assessment
Spelling Test

Correlating the two blank lines of the reading and spelling tests given on page 43 of this book will give you a profile of the letter patterns with which your student is experiencing difficulty These should be remediated before continuing in this book. If your student has not completed *Book 5* you should begin with the assessment tests on pages 37–38 of that book, to check that your student is operating at the correct level for him/her.

Top blank line –   Note any incorrect spellings form Section 1, page 43 on this line.

Lower blank line – Note any word read incorrectly on the Reading Test in Section 2 on page 43.

1 athlete	2 remained	3 highlight	4 headline	5 motherland
_____	_____	_____	_____	_____
_____	_____	_____	_____	_____
complete	maintain	skylight	deadly	smother
6 snowbound	**7** feeble	**8** beautiful	**9** centigrade	**10** cycle
_____	_____	_____	_____	_____
_____	_____	_____	_____	_____
snowdrift	steeple	beauty	celery	cyclonic
11 recent	**12** overture	**13** gentlemen	**14** loud	**15** gin
_____	_____	_____	_____	_____
_____	_____	_____	_____	_____
centrally	premature	generation	proud	ginger
16 knowing	**17** gracefully	**18** boatyard	**19** flirting	**20** matchbox
_____	_____	_____	_____	_____
_____	_____	_____	_____	_____
unknown	bracing	boathouse	skirting	scratched

The Lessons

Check your skills

You will need a pencil, your exercise book, a dictionary, and a stopwatch.

1. Copy the following sentence in your exercise book.

   The quick brown fox jumps over the lazy dog.

2. Time yourself filling in the Long Vowel Choices Chart on page 225.

   ___minutes ____seconds

   If you have not used *Book 5*, study the LVCC on page 226 and practice completing it using the puzzle pieces found on pages 227–228 which were introduced in *Books 4* and *5*.

3. Do you remember the rules for syllable dividing?
   Complete these sentences:

   Rule 1 Split between_____ (i.e., rabbit)

   Rule 2 If only one consonant split before the _____ (i.e., robot)

   Rule 3 If this does not work divide_____ (i.e., robin)

4. Split the words below into syllables and then time yourself looking them up in a dictionary:

   nutmeg

   halo

   supplement

   vitamin

   [___minutes ___seconds]

Check your skills, continued

1. Listen to the teacher. (See page 14.) Your teacher will give you 20 words to spell. Write them in your exercise book.

   Listen carefully.

   Don't forget to write one syllable at a time.

2. Read these words to your teacher.
   (Teacher notes any incorrect responses on the Record Sheet, found on page 39, comparing them with the spelling test in Section 1.)

1. complete	2. maintain
3. skylight	4. deadly
5. smother	6. snowdrift
7. steeple	8. beauty
9. celery	10. cyclonic
11. centrally	12. premature
13. generation	14. proud
15. ginger	16. unknown
17. bracing	18. boathouse
19. skirting	20. scratched

1. Work with a friend. In your exercise book write a word spelled with any of the patterns below. You may draw one line from ○ to ○ for each correctly spelled word. If your line completes a rectangle, you may claim it by signing your initials in it. The winner is the one with the most completed rectangles.

-ic	-ture	ea e	ea E
e - e	ai	-tion	ou
o U	-ble	-fle	-tle
-zle	-cle	-kle	-dle
-gle	-ple	igh	-ice
-age	ough	ou ow	ow
oa	-ir	-tch	ar

Punctuate and add capital letters to the first three paragraphs of the following passage:

do you fancy tracking animals through the stark beauty of the african wilderness if you have not been to south africa it is the holiday of a lifetime a safari in africa is an experience that no other holiday can equal

1

i once visited an african game reserve called kruger national park we approached the camp in an open-topped land rover along a dirt track leaving clouds of dust behind us our accommodation at

2

mopani tree lodge was in thatched wooden huts which were constructed in the trees they had no windows so the top half of the walls was open to the sights and sounds of africa thomas our game ranger woke us before sunrise to go on our first game spotting expedition

3

✂ -

it is hard to describe the thrill of waking to the sounds and smells of the african bush viewing the wonderful spectacle of the african giants the bright plumage of the birds the african thorn trees and all the other amazing flora and fauna

4

Eating your dinner around a huge log fire in the center of the boma (a circular wooden stockade) with lanterns hanging from the trees is magical. The African star-spangled sky is above your head. The Milky Way stretches banner-like across it with the Southern Cross

5

and the dazzlingly bright planet of Jupiter shining down upon you. It is an unforgettable experience. You are not allowed to make your way back to your sleeping quarters unescorted. You must be accompanied by a game ranger in case there are any wild animals roaming in the vicinity, looking for a quick snack.

6

Nothing can compare with the thrill of the very first encounter with these wonderful animals in their natural habitat. When your ranger gets the message that a pride of lions has just been seen down by the waterhole, the thrill of the chase is paramount. You suddenly depart from the rough track and shoot across the scrub, ducking from the grasp of the overhead branches of the thorn trees as you go.

7

In the last paragraphs:

1. Underline or highlight 5 verbs in red, 5 adjectives in blue, 2 adverbs in orange and 2 prepositions in yellow.

2. Underline ten suffixes in black.

3. Name the "big five" African animals which you think most people would want to see.

Vowel pattern ur

Don't h**ur**t me, N**ur**se.

1. Auditory Introduction. (See page 13.)
2. Visual Introduction. (See page 13.)
3. Introduce the clueword and Reading/Spelling Cards.
4. Say **nurse** **e r**. The sound is the same as **herb** **e r** **girl** **e r**.

5. Highlight the **ur** and practice reading these words. When you are ready, read the words to your teacher.

hurt	church	burp	burn	curb
fur	turn	burst	curl	absurd
urban	turban	surplus	burden	gurgle

6. Listen as your teacher gives you some words. (See page 14.) Write **ur** in the box if you hear **e r** in the word.

1	2	3	4	5	6	7	8

More about vowel pattern ur

1. Underline **ur** e r . You should find eleven.

Thursdaymorningisurgentlyusedforburningrubbishensuring

thatgermsdonoteverturninthespurninghurtingtheherbsin

urbanurnstrundlingcursorcurds

2. Each of the words below is missing an **ur**. Fill in the **ur** and read each word to your teacher.

n____se [   ]   c____ve [   ]   p____se [   ]

b____st [   ]   ret____ning [   ]   sp____n [   ]

ch____ch [   ]   p____ge [   ]   m____derer [   ]

dist____bing [   ]   bl____b [   ]   b____ning [   ]

Th____sday [   ]   h____tful [   ]   g____gle [   ]

Count the number of syllables in each word and write the number in the brackets after each word.

3. Draw a picture to go with each of the words below. Consult your dictionary if you don't know the meaning of the words.

burst	curve	urn	hurdle

More about vowel pattern ur

1. Use the words in the right hand column to complete the sentences:

1. He _____ when he realized that he had a _____ tire. He pulled off the road to change the wheel.

burst   cursed

2. The _____ _____ him when she gave him an _____.

nurse injection
hurt

3. The _____ took care not to _____ the _____ when he _____ for the jewels on _____.

Thursday
disturb burglar
furniture returned

4. The _____ twisted and _____ as the _____ waves _____ him towards the shore.

hurled surfer
turned surging

1. Read

It was a murky night at Hurst Castle, the residence of the Burton family. Burl had found an old hurdy-gurdy in the east wing, which some ancestor must have purchased at one time. Pushing back the furniture, his friends began hurling themselves around the floor in time to its lively music.

Soon it was all getting out of hand and Burl wished that his father would intervene and curtail the wild proceedings before anyone got hurt.

Unfortunately, Dad was in his study working away at the latest novel he was writing. Scribbling frantically, with a burst of inspiration, he was working out a strategy for the disposal of the body of the murder victim. He had decided that the body would be cast into the turgid waters of the creek, and this is what he wrote:

continued on next page

"Taking a furtive look over his shoulder, the scoundrel carried the sturdy body of the girl across the meadow and hurled it into the creek. The corpse's yellow curls and purple gown were soon immersed in the churning waters, where it was carried off by the strong current. Further downstream the creek curved, turning into a huge dam, in whose depths the body would be swallowed up."

Putting down his pen, feeling pleased with himself now that he had disposed of the body, Lord Burton helped himself to a drink and put his feet up for a break before he tackled the next episode of the tale.

2. What do you think happened next? Put your answer on the computer, write it in your exercise book, or record it on tape.

Vowel pattern **er, ir, ur** choices

he**rb**   **g**i**rl**   **n**u**rse**   The letters **er**, **ir**, and **ur** all have the same sound **e r**.

1. Read the words below carefully, underlining the **e r** spelling pattern. Splitting the words into syllables will help with the difficult words.

curb dessert immerse insertion verb skirt swerve furniture circle stirring squirt circumstances submerge disturbed blurted slur circulation refurbish herded turn

2. Now complete these sentences (all the words are from Section 1, but only refer to it if necessary).
   1. A _____ is a doing or action word.
   2. Owls can _____ their heads around almost full _____ .
   3. Under the _____ the driver did well to _____ so as not to crash the vehicle onto the _____ which would have been a disaster for the people standing at the bus stop.
   4. The young sailor was _____ by his first experience in the submarine as the command was given for it to _____ .
   5. _____ the pudding is fun. One can then look forward to eating it with a _____ of cream for _____ .

3. Glue the Sound Picture words below onto a card and then cut them out. Shuffle them and then arrange them correctly under the three headings **er**, **ir**, and **ur**. Ask your teacher to check your work.

s l er	**s k er t**	**k er b**	**k er v**
s k er m i sh	**s er v a nt**	**er j e nt l E**	
s er ow nd	**d E z er t**	**s er v i s**	
s er k'l	**s kw er t e d**	**st er i ng**	
b l er t e d	**i m er s**	**s u b m er j**	

Now write the correct spellings clearly, in pencil, on the back of each card. Use the words you found hard to spell in written sentences in your exercise book. Be sure to spell the words correctly.

4. Ask your teacher for a spelling test. (See page 14.) Write the words in your exercise book.

Homework planning

Don't let the threat of homework spoil your life! Careful planning and management of the time available to you will mean you can be sure of getting it all done and still have time to do the things you want to do!

1. Copy the Homework Plan into your notebook and fill it in for every evening that you have homework this week. It will help you to organize your time. You may find that you need to allow more time than you thought for certain subjects. If there is a problem discuss it with the teacher for that subject.

Homework Plan

	Subject	Estimated time	Actual time
1.	_____	_____	_____
2.	_____	_____	_____
3.	_____	_____	_____
4.	_____	_____	_____
5.	_____	_____	_____

Homework planning, continued

Devise your own weekly homework plan based on what you have discovered by using the Homework Plan on page 55. You may need to discuss this with your parents and teachers first. Remember to include short intervals for rest and relaxation throughout the evening. It is impossible to work effectively without them.

Time (Change these times to suit you)	Monday	Tuesday	Wednesday	Thursday	Friday
4:00–4:30	after school				
4:30–5:00	football				
5:00–5:30	travel home				
5:30–6:00	relax T.V.				
6:00–6:30	supper				
6:30–7:15	English				
7:15–7:30	rest				
7:30–8:00	French				
8:00–8:30	math				
8:30–9:00	relax T.V.				
9:00–9:30	bath + bed				

Vowel pattern oy

R**oy** ann**oy**s the b**oy**.

1. Auditory Introduction. (See page 13.)
2. Visual Introduction. (See page 13.)
3. Introduce the clueword and Reading/Spelling Cards.
4. Say **boy o y**. **oy** occurs most often as a final syllable in words.

5. Highlight the **oy** and practice reading these words. When you are ready, read the words to your teacher.

boy	coy	toy	soy	joy
employ	oyster	destroy	enjoy
annoy	convoy	decoy	alloy

6. Listen as your teacher gives you some words. (See page 14.) Write **oy** in the box if you hear **o y** at the end of the word.

1	2	3	4	5	6	7	8	9	10

More about vowel pattern oy

1. Each of the words below is missing the **oy**. Fill in the **oy** and read each word to your teacher.

j_____   dec_____   pl_____

ann_____   t_____   all_____

Tr_____   destr_____   empl_____

2. **oy** occurs at the end of a syllable and is often the final syllable in a word. Sometimes it occurs at the end of a syllable but in the middle of a word. Example: **loy al**. Remember this as you fill in the puzzle.

1. Affectedly shy or modest

2. A cunning trick

3. Mix of 2 or more metals

4. To give a job to someone

5. To break up, demolish

6. To do with a king or queen

7. Doing something happily

8. A kind of bean

9. A trip, usually by the sea

10. Faithfulness

More about vowel pattern oy

1. Underline or highlight the **o y** pattern in these words.

   1. Example: <u>co</u>y   <u>jo</u>y   (jay)   <u>to</u>y

   2.   envoy   replay   enjoy   convoy

   3.   annoy   ahoy   alloy   away

   4.   Goya   royal   loyal   relay

   5.   foyer   employer   player   destroyer

   6.   destroy   decay   deploy   decoy

   Circle the word in each group that is different. Read all the words.

2. Dictionary Exercises:

   All the words in the following two lists have the same first three letters.
   Arrange them in dictionary order in your exercise book according to their
   fourth letters.

   1. decide   decoy   decrease   decay   declaim
      deck   decent

   2. consult   conceal condition   confess convoy
      contest   conical

   Look up the following words in your dictionary. Underline the word which is
   not an animal.

   coypu   coyote   hoyden

More about vowel pattern oy

1. Read and underline or highlight the **oy** pattern. You should find 14.
   Practice reading this story several times. When you are ready, read it to your teacher. Your teacher will give you the whole story or a few sentences from the story as a dictation exercise. Please write your dictation in your exercise book.

The flamboyant Mr. Doyle was standing in the foyer of the Savoy Hotel when he saw his pride and joy, his silver Rolls Royce zoom past the door. He rushed out to see joyriders driving off towards the highway. He was so annoyed that he could no longer enjoy his dish of oysters and went to alert the police. They soon informed him that the car had been destroyed in a crash. The joyriders, who were unemployed, were already at the Croydon Police Station and under arrest.

What do you call a boy who swims around in circles in rivers?   Eddy.

Brilliant video words

(Student and teacher read together.)

1. Do you remember the rules for splitting words into syllables?

   1. Split between two consonants **vc/cv**. Example: rab/bit

   2. If only one consonant, split **v/cv** before the consonant. Example: ro/bot

   3. If this does not make a sensible word split **vc/v** after the consonant. Example: rob/in

   You are now going to learn the 4th way to split syllables.

   4. Between two vowels which do not combine to make one sound, split **v/v**. Example: Stu/art

   Note: tr<u>ai</u>l tri/al   l<u>oi</u>n li/on   d<u>ai</u>r/y di/ar/y

   Split and read the following words **v/v**.

Example: ri/ot	Romeo	studio	audience
duel	quiet	rodeo	audio	medium
fuel	client	radio	senior	secretarial
cruel	video	ratio	chariot	experience
duet	union	patio	diamond	immediate
diet	onion	folio	museum	

2. Now show that you know which rule applies by putting the number of the rule (1, 2, 3, or 4) in brackets dividing the words into syllables according to the rules in Section 1.

   stuc/co [1]   (v c / c v)

   bi/ped [2]   (v c v)

   Borneo [   ]

   junior [   ]

   banjo [   ]

   cabinet [   ]

   brandish [   ]

   rodeo [   ]

   Ronda [   ]

   cable [   ]

   garage [   ]

   tonic [   ]

   burden [   ]

   parish [   ]

   charter [   ]

   porridge [   ]

   banish [   ]

   follow [   ]

1. Make the singular nouns into plural nouns in the following passage. What else do you need to change when you do this?

The "Food Program" suggests that if you like eating a really good tomato, you ought to travel to a Mediterranean country where this produce is eaten daily. The taste of this crop, grown in a sunny region, has no resemblance to the bland product we are used to buying in our local super-market. If you live in Great Britain and are a potato

enthusiast you will be delighted to know that Scotland grows the best potato in Europe. The colder climate produces a better crop in this instance. The tomato cargo changes hands in the European marketplace. If you compare a photo of a tomato grown in the UK during a hot season with one grown in a poor season it will show that quantity and quality improve in a hot summer.

Writing for a purpose: A business letter

1. Use this business letter format to present the contents of the letter of complaint found in Section 2. Write each part in the appropriate section or paragraph on the lined paper provided on page 64. Remember a paragraph is a group of sentences about the same topic and each paragraph starts on a new line. (Teacher and student may read the contents of the business letter together.)

Your address

Name + address of company to whom you are writing

Date

Greeting,

Subject

Paragraph 1 Introduce the content of the letter and explain why you are writing.

Paragraph 2 Write the main subject matter of the letter.

Concluding paragraph Summarize and indicate the response you would like to receive.

Saluations,

Signature

2. Top Trees, 224 Fieldhead Lane, Centercity, Minnesota 55333 Burnford and Company, Middleton, Iowa 66222 November 16, 2000 Dear Sir, Subject: Bicycle gears – Model Road Ranger 11. I am sorry to have to write and complain about the gears on the bicycle I purchased only a month ago, which was manufactured by your company. The gears have always been difficult to use but yesterday I could not select any gears at all. When I tried to change gears, there was a nasty grinding noise and the chain fell off. This was very irritating and should not happen on a model which cost $450, especially as you advertise the bicycle as having "quick, easy gear changes" and "having the flexibility of 21 different speeds available at the touch of a lever." I have taken it back to your agent in Iowa, but he told me that there was nothing he could do and suggested that I contact you. I should be pleased to have an early reply with your suggestions as I need the machine to enable me to travel to school and back. Yours faithfully, Your Name

Business letter

_____

_____

_____

_____

_____

_____

_____

_____

_____

_____

_____

_____

_____

_____

_____

_____

_____

_____

_____

_____

_____

_____

_____

Vowel pattern oi

"**Oi, oi**! Lend me a c**oi**n, Mate."

1. Auditory Introduction. (See page 13.)
2. Visual Introduction. (See page 13.)
3. Introduce the clueword and Reading/Spelling Cards.
4. Say **coin** **o y** . **oi** occurs as the beginning or main syllable of a word. What other letter team makes the same sound?

5. Highlight the **oi** and practice reading these words. When you are ready, read the words to your teacher.

broil	moist	soil	choice	void
oil	coil	joint	toil	coin
join	noise	boil	spoil	sirloin

6. Listen as your teacher gives you some words. (See page 14.) Write **oi** in the box if you hear **o y** in the word.

1	2	3	4	5	6	7	8	9	10

More about vowel pattern oi

1. Each of the words below is missing the **oi**. Fill in the **oi** and read each word to your teacher.

   b_____l   sp_____led   rec_____led

   embr_____dery   unav_____dable

   disapp_____ntment   expl_____ted

2. Highlight the **oi** pattern in these words. Circle the word in each group that does not rhyme. Read the words to your teacher.

   1. join   groin   groan   loin   coin
   2. foil   toil   soil   foal   oil   boil
   3. joist   moist   foist   joust
   4. choice   voice   rejoice   chance

3. Read.

   Friendship Poem

   There's good mates and bad mates
   'sorry to keep you waiting mates
   Cheap skates and wet mates
   The ones you end up hating mates
   Hard mates and fighting mates
   Witty and exciting mates
   Mates you want to hug
   And mates you want to clout
   Ones that get you into trouble
   And ones that get you out.

   by Roger McGough

Crossword fun oi

Remember that each answer contains an **oi** pattern.

Read and then choose from these words to complete the crossword.

turmoil	joiner	exploit	moist	foible
anoint	spoil	Polaroid	goiter	appointment
hoist	loiter	soil	boil	sirloin
poison	oil	toil	tabloid	hoick
noise	voice	doily	void	mastoid
ointment	turquoise	poise	point	cloisters

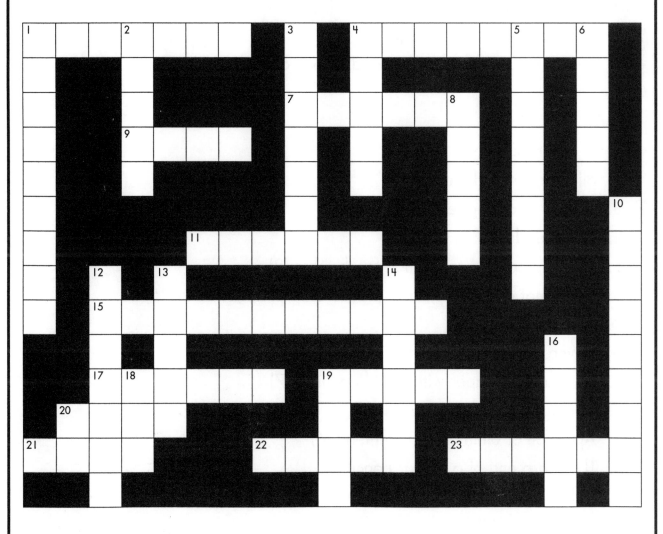

Clues to complete the crossword puzzle are found on page 68.

Crossword fun clues

Across

1. Agitation or state of disorder (7)
4. Camera which produces a finished print rapidly (8)
7. Harmful substance (6)
9. Upper layer of ground in which plants grow (4)
11. Swelling in the neck as a result of enlargement of the thyroid gland (6)
15. Arrangement to meet at a specific time and place (11)
17. To hang about or linger doing nothing (6)
19. Sound formed in the larynx, used for singing, shouting, speaking (5)
20. Work incessantly (4)
21. When a liquid starts to bubble up (4)
22. Raise by means of ropes (5)
23. Person who makes furniture and woodwork (6)

Down

1. A bluish stone (9)
2. Slightly wet or damp (5)
3. A bold or daring feat (7)
4. Composed manner (5)
5. Greasy healing preparation for the skin (8)
6. Small mat of paper or lace, placed on a plate for cakes (5)
8. A sound (5)
10. Covered walks in convents or cathedrals (9)
12. Popular newspaper with bold headlines (7)
13. Damage or allow to go bad (5)
14. Apply oil or ointment at ceremony (6)
16. The sharp end of a tool or pencil (5)
18. To lubricate; gasoline is refined from it (3)
19. Empty, vacant (4)
20. I went _ _ the shop (2)

More about oy and oi

1. Fill in **oi** or **oy** and read:

R___ was on the b___l and sp___ling for a fight. When Tom
Benton, the j___ner, arrived late for his app___ntment with his
empl___er, R___ was very ann___ed.

"You're a sp___led, lazy b___, Tom," stormed R___ , in his
h___ty-t___ty v___ce.

"If you disapp___nt me again, I'll have no ch___ce but to sack
you."

"I could help you h___st that j ___st, R___ ," said Tom, in a
quiet v___ce, hoping to av___d the sack.

"That's not the p___nt," said R___ , n___ sily, beads of
m___sture breaking out on his brow. But he could see that the
b___ was l___al. "Oh, go and shift that heap of s___beans."

- Notice that quotation marks are wrapped around the words which are
  actually spoken.
- Note the position of periods and commas when quotation marks are used.
- Notice that each time another person speaks a new line is used.

Writing a letter of application

1.

| Looking for summer employment?
The Royal Hotel

requires extra waiting staff for the summer. Smart appearance and pleasant manner important. Must live locally.

Apply in writing to: Mrs. S. Royston, The Royal Hotel, Cliff Dr., Seatown, MA 02134 | **R.W. Wood**
Joiners

require an Apprentice 16/17 years old Day release for college. Must be eager to learn a trade.

Write to: R. Wood Esq., 13, Hill St., Seatown, MA 02134 |

Write a letter of application for one of these jobs which were advertised in the Seatown Gazette on May 17th. First write a rough draft giving personal details about yourself. Write in paragraphs. Look at the letter you wrote on page 64, and think carefully about how to format your letter. Now make a neat copy.

Long vowel pattern ie

Good gr**ie**f! Big ch**ie**f.

1. Auditory Introduction. (See page 13.)
2. Visual Introduction. (See page 13.)
3. Introduce the clueword and Reading/Spelling Cards.
4. Say **chief** **E** . The sound is the same as alphabetical name **E** .
   The pattern **ie** is the 4th spelling choice for the **E** sound in the main part
   of a word.

5. Highlight the **ie** and practice reading these words. When you are ready, read
   the words to your teacher.

shield	priest	yield	pier	siege
chief	thief	brief	piece	grieve
field	niece	fierce	pierce	shriek
believe	cashier	diesel	retrieve	belief

6. Listen as your teacher gives you some words. (See page 14.) Write **ie** in the
   box if you hear **E** in the word.

1	2	3	4	5	6	7	8

More about long vowel pattern ie

1. Highlight all the words which have the **ie** pattern. Read all the words to your teacher.

siege	these	fierce	freeze	briefcase
thieves	three	hygienic	believable	peach
breve	stream	cheap	chief	field
grieving	yeast	achieve	priest	cheat
niece	pierced	theme	shriek	yield
diesel	retriever	relieved	piercing	peace
repeat	masterpiece		achievement	reprieve

2. Join the letters to write the words.

th
gr
br
bel
rel
> ief

Example: _____thief_____

_____

_____

_____

_____

sh
f
y
w
> ield

_____

_____

_____

_____

3. Copy the headings below into your exercise book. Listen as your teacher gives you a list of words from section 1. All the words have an **E▶** sound. Write each word in the correct column.

Long Vowel Sound Picture	Main part of word			
	1st try	2nd try	3rd try	4th try
E▶	ee	ea	e – e	ie
	Examples: teeth	scream	delete	field

More about long vowel pattern ie

1. Use the words in the word bank to complete these sentences.

   1. Although they had been under _____ for three months, the people inside the castle would not _____ .

   2. My _____ has had her ears and nose _____ .

   3. The _____ family was comforted by the Roman Catholic _____ .

   4. The _____ of police was _____ to hear that his force had escaped the latest terrorist attack.

   5. A golden _____ is not a very _____ dog.

   6. The truck runs on _____ , not gasoline.

   7. He had the artist's _____ in his _____ .

   8. The report that the judge had granted a _____ to the violent _____ was frankly un_____ .

   9. Wear a coat so you do not _____ .

believable		**Word Bank**		retriever
grieving	fierce	niece	diesel	reprieve
yield	siege	masterpiece	pierced	priest
relieved	chief	briefcase	freeze	thieves

2. Your teacher will give you four sentences from Section 1 for dictation. Write your dictation in your exercise book.

More about long vowel pattern ie

1. Look at your new card for **E**. You have now learned a 4th way to spell **E** in the main part of a word and 5 ways in total. Look at the Long Vowel Choices Chart.

Long Vowel Sound Picture	Open syllable	Main part of word				End of the word One syllable word	
		1st try	2nd try	3rd try	4th try	4th try	1st try
	E	**E**	**E**	**E**	**E**	**E**	**E**
E	e	ee	ea	e-e	ie	ee	ea
	equals	queen	cream	athlete	chief	bee	tea

2. Link the rhyming pairs.

grieves	fierce
believed	piece
frieze	chiefly
yielding	relieved
niece	thieves
pierce	shielding
briefly	seize

3. Find the **E** puzzle piece on page 228, cut it out, and place it on the Long Vowel Choices Chart.

E
ie
chief

What did the priest say when he saw insects on his flowers?

Let us spray.

Proofreading

1. This account was written by a boy on return from Cub camp. It is going to be printed in the Cub Newsletter and it is your job to rewrite it correctly before it is published.

- Read and underline all spelling mistakes.
- Add any periods and mark capital letters.
- Divide it into paragraphs and mark the end of each paragraph like this // .
  A paragraph is a group of sentences about the same idea or topic.
  Each new paragraph starts on a new line.
- Now rewrite it neatly using correct spellings and punctuation and dividing it into paragraphs.

Example: after <u>brefast,</u> we <u>packt</u> <u>are</u> bags and went to <u>are</u>

next desterneshon which was two miuls away. our cub leder

said it woud tack us one houer to get there but we thurt it

woud tack longer and we sat of. It did onley tack one

houwer wen we got there we pichid are tants. we pich are

tents quily so we had time to go for a walk wich we did not

like but we made a deul that id we went for a walk we coud

have a camp firere that night. the walk was not to long and

we got are bages for walking tow miuls and at lest we had

someone to tuke to. it was nerly tow oklok so we had some

lunch. We did do some archarey and afletics cloesly

supavised untill five oklok. we had a bit of a shock at five

oklok because a sponserd walk came righgt thuw were are

tents were pichid so we have to move are tents. Bay the time

we moved are tents it was gating dark and we had a camp

firer and the club leder had some march malos we cookt

them on the bon fier. Than we had a game of football in the

dark then we protendid to gow to slep. Wen the cub leder

had gon we snuk out and got up to some mifchif. We got

back in to are tents an houer or sow later then we gust torkt

for the rest of the night.

Compare your proofreading with the corrected account to be found in the
teacher's notes.(See page 31.) Make a note of any spelling mistakes you
failed to spot and learn how to spell the word(s) correctly.

Long vowel pattern ie

This pie chart shows how Floyd spent $1.20.

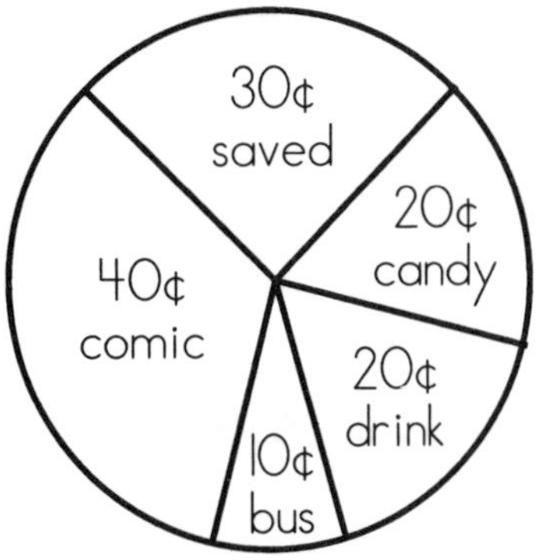

A p**ie**ce of p**ie**.

Make a pie chart to show how you spent $2.40.

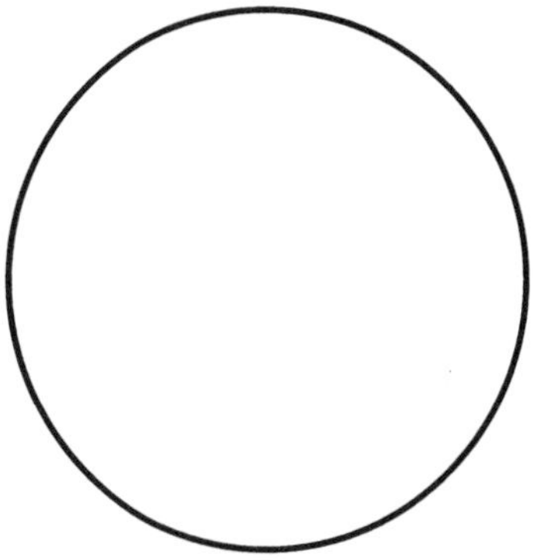

1. Auditory Introduction. (See page 13.)
2. Visual Introduction. (See page 13.)
3. Introduce the clueword and Reading/Spelling Cards.
4. Say **pie** I. The sound is the same as alphabetical name I.
   The pattern **ie** is the 3rd choice for spelling I at the end of words.

5. Highlight the **ie** and practice reading these words. When you are ready, read the words to your teacher.

die	tie	pie	lie	fie
magpies	vie	untie	died	

Plurals:

cry	cries	sky	skies
spy	spies	fly	flies

6. Listen as your teacher gives you some words. (See page 14.) Write **ie** in the box if you hear I at the end of the word.

1	2	3	4	5	6	7	8

More about long vowel pattern ie

1. Complete each sentence.

died   lie   vie   tie   pie

1. Do you like pumpkin _____?

2. Did Floyd tell a _____?

3. The boys_____ with each other to see who is the strongest.

4. He _____ in a train crash last year.

5. Can you _____ her shoelaces please?

2. Copy these headings for **I▶** as the end part of a word in your exercise book. Listen your teacher read some words. Write them in the correct column.

-y	-igh	ie

3. Look at your new spelling card for **I▶**. You have now learned a 3rd way to spell **I▶** at the end of words. You now know 5 ways to spell the **I▶** sound.

Long Vowel Sound Picture	Open syllable	Main part of word		End of the word One syllable word		
		1st try	2nd try	1st try	2nd try	3rd try
I	v c v c i iron	i-e smile	igh night	y cry	igh high	ie pie

I▶
ie
pie

Handwriting Practice
Trace and copy.

ur   nurse

Turkey for dinner for the third time!

oy   Roy

The royal family enjoys much loyalty.

oi   noise

The cloisters rang with voices rejoicing.

ie   thief

The chief gets the biggest piece of pie.

Mr.   Mrs.   Miss   Ms.

Dr.   Prof.   Rev.   Col.

Someone who is grieving is full of grief.

The United Kingdom is also Great Britain.

Did you see the brilliant video on lions?

Looking at plurals

1. For some words which end in **f** or **ff** just add **s** to form the plural.

   Example: cliffs   roofs   chiefs

   Usually **f** changes to **v** and **es** is added. Add **s** or **es** to the words.

   wife_____   thief_____   shelf _____   calf _____

   life _____   loaf_____   self _____   half_____

   sniff_____   wolf_____   leaf_____   chief _____

2. Normally nouns ending in **o** add **es** to form the plural.

   Example: cargo – cargoes

   Match the singular to the plural in the columns below.

   potato   vetoes   gringo   manifestoes
   tomato   radios   embargo   cameos
   radio   potatoes   folio   heroes
   photo   rodeos   torpedo   folios
   rodeo   tomatoes   manifesto   gringos
   video   photos   hero   embargoes
   veto   videos   cameo   torpedoes

   Which nouns are the exception to the rule? _____

   _____

3. Irregular plural forms. A small number of nouns do not conform to any rules about forming the plural. See if you can match these irregular plurals.

Singular (only one)	**Plural (more than one)**
man	women
goose	teeth
child	lice
tooth	dice
foot	oxen
woman	mice
louse	geese
ox	feet
die	men
mouse	children

Abbreviations

An abbreviation is a way of shortening the written form of a word.

1. We often use short forms for the days of the week and months of the year.
   Complete:

   Example: Sept. _____September_____   Sat. _____
              Oct. _____   Tues. _____
              Feb. _____   Thur. _____ | Take note of the periods |
              Jan. _____   Wed. _____
              Aug. _____   Fri. _____

2. Points of the compass. Write the full name of each direction.

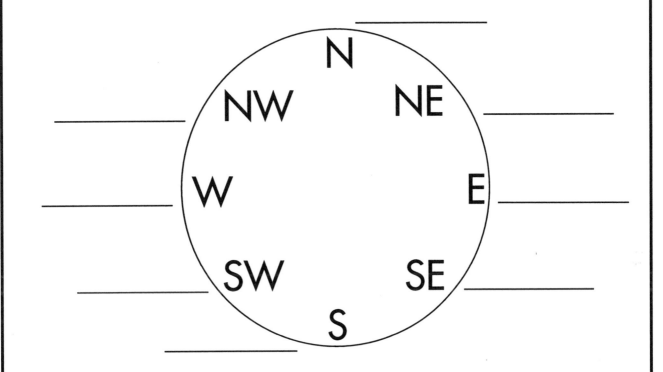

3. Titles can be abbreviated. Match these abbreviations to their words.

   Example: P.D.   Mister

            Prof.   Doctor

            Mr.   Police Department

            Rev.   Professor

            Dr.   Captain

            Capt.   Reverend

More about abbreviations

1. Abbreviations are used in addresses and occupations. Join these to their words.

La.	Park	St.	Gardens
Gr.	Drive	Rd.	Street
Dr.	Lane	Sq.	Road
Pk.	Green	Gdns.	Square
R.N.	Registered Nurse	D.D.S.	Doctor of Dentistry

2. Units of measurement of weight, length, volume, and time are often abbreviated. Join these.

lb	centimeter	sec.	cubic centimeter
ml	kilogram	cc	ante meridiem
cm	milliliter	min.	post meridiem
kg	kilometer	p.m.	second
km	pound	a.m.	minute

3. Can you guess these frequently used abbreviations?
Write the word(s) for each.

U.S.A._____

S.A.E._____

M.P.H._____

U.N._____

A.S.A.P._____

R.S.V.P._____

4. Telephone directories and maps make use of abbreviations because of a lack of space. Can you work out the full addresses and occupations of these people? Tell your teacher.

K.J. Lloyd Dent. Surg., 632 Heathfield Pl., Atlanta GA
R.T. Burton Newsagts., 42 Princess Dr., Detroit, Mich.
F.L. Murdock Eng., The Beeches, Brook Sq., Lakeville, VT
Dr. T.G. Boothroyd J.P., 55 Westmoor Gdns., Cherry Creek, Nev.

5. Listen to your teacher read some words. (See page 14.) Write them as abbreviations in your exercise book. Cover this page and test yourself on what you have learned.

Vowel digraph pattern au

Astron**au**ts like s**au**ce!

1. Auditory Introduction. (See page 13.)
2. Visual Introduction. (See page 13.)
3. Introduce the clueword and Reading/Spelling Cards.
4. Say **sauce** `aw`. Vowel pattern **au** in words says `aw`.

5. Highlight the **au** and practice reading these words. When you are ready, read the words to your teacher.

sauce	taut	haul	maul	fault	cause
pause	launch	faucet	fraud	haunts	gaunt
flaunt	paunch	pause	gauze	vault	because
caused	autumn	laundry	gaudy	fauna	applause
traumatic		inaudible		authority	jaundice

6. Listen as your teacher gives you some words. (See page 15.) Write **au** in the box if you hear `aw` in the word.

1	2	3	4	5	6	7	8

More about au

1. These words are missing the **au**. Write **au** on each line and practice reading the words. Read them to your teacher and then write the words in your exercise book as a spelling test.

t_____nt   tr_____ma   p_____se

fl_____nt   v_____lt   d_____nt

cl_____se   l_____nch   bec_____se

h_____nt   h_____l   g_____dy

2. Complete these sentences. Read the sentences to your teacher and be ready for some dictation. Write the sentences in your exercise book.

vault   applause   haunts

traumatic   laundry   fraud

launch   sauce   autumn

1. They will _____ the rocket at the beginning of _____ in order to make use of the best weather conditions.

2. The _____ squad traced the missing money to a _____ in an offshore bank.

3. The audience gave the performers a loud round of _____.

4. The memory of the _____ accident still _____ Paul.

More about vowel digraph pattern au

1. Here is a recipe for you to try for Simple Curry Sauce. This can be used for meat, fish, or vegetable dishes.

Ingredients:

2 ounces margarine

1 onion

1 apple

1 tablespoon flour

1 tablespoon curry powder

1 teaspoon curry paste (optional)

500 ml (1 pint) stock (Use meat stock for meat curries, fish stock for fish, and yeast extract for vegetable or egg curries.)

salt, pepper, and 1 teaspoon sugar

1 dessert spoon desiccated coconut

1 tablespoon raisins

1 tablespoon chutney

a few drops of vinegar or lemon

You will find it easier to follow this recipe if you add the punctuation first. Curries are a good way to use up leftovers.

Method:

Heat the margarine and fry the finely chopped onion and apple stir until soft stir in the flour and curry powder cook gently for several minutes gradually add the stock and bring to a boil cook this until it has thickened then add the remaining ingredients taste the sauce to make sure there is enough seasoning and sweetening add the food to be curried and simmer until well cooked raw meat may take several hours cook fish raw vegetables or cooked meat for 25 to 30 minutes serve with cooked rice chutney and side dishes such as sliced banana cucumber tomato and celery.

More about vowel digraph pattern au

1. Listen to the teacher. (See page 15.) Don't confuse **ou** saying **ow** and **au** saying **aw**. Underline or highlight the word you hear.

   1. sound   launch   sauce   lunch   loud

   2. pause   clause   cloud   flaunt   flounce

   3. paunch   pouch   laundry   foundry   launder

   4. applause   applied   around   automatic   autocratic

   5. taut   tout   trout   hound   haunt

2. Listen to the teacher. (See page 15.) Write each word under the heading **ou** **ow** or **au** **aw**. There will be 5 words under each heading.

   ou **ow**   **au** **aw**

   _____   _____

   _____   _____

   _____   _____

   _____   _____

   _____   _____

3. Read these words. Highlight each **gh**.

   gh is silent: caught   taught   haughty   naughty   daughter   slaughter

   Odd word: LAUGH – HA! HA!

When does an astronaut have his midday meal?   At launch time.   R|S

Looking at words with prefixes and suffixes

1. Add the prefix **re**, **dis**, or **ex** to change the meaning of these words and trace over the letters. Read the words you have made.

____ grace	____ plain	____ main
____ array	____ claim	____ play
____ train	____ place	____ pay

2. Read the words and then underline the prefixes.

unequal	concave	mischief	injustice
explain	illegal	impossible	interact
superimpose	proposition	irregular	disloyal

3. Trace and add consonant suffixes **-able, -ful**, **-ly**, **-ment**, or **-ness** to these words. Read.

train____	bold____	elope____	slow____
narrow____	boast____	dole____	close____
whole____	enroll____	shallow____	encroach____

4. Add vowel suffixes **-ing**, **-er**, **-able**, or **-ed** to these words and write the words you make on the lines below. Remember the silent "**e**" spelling rules. Read the words.

advise	light	vie	ride
_____	_____	_____	_____
prize	untie	drive	entwine
_____	_____	_____	_____
desire	die	decide	frighten
_____	_____	_____	_____

Reading and completing words

1. Cross off a letter pattern when you have used it to complete a word in the passage.

a-e	-ce	ic	-le	ou ou ou ou	u-e
-age -age	-dge	-ice	oa	ow	ur ur ur
ai	ea ea ea ea	i-e	o-e o-e o-e	oy oy	-y
ar	ee ee	ie	oi	-tch	
au	er er er er	-igh -igh	oo oo oo oo	-tion	
ay	-ge	ir ir	or or or	-ture	

M _ st _ _ y begins on Octob _ _ 31st. I had to take a pizza to Bri _ _ _ Cott _ _ _ . When I got to the pla _ _ which was written on the p _ _ ce of pap _ _ , it l _ _ ked l _ k _ it was abandoned. I knocked on the old _ _ k d _ _ r, but no one c _ m _ . I knocked again and I was ab _ _ t to go when a f _ _ nt v _ _ ce said,

"Who's there?"

I said, "The pizza man."

This litt _ _ b _ _ answered the door. He asked, "H _ _ much is it, pl _ _ se?"

So I answered in a s _ _ prised voice, "$10.50. That incl _ d _ s garl _ _ br _ _ d and two pizzas at $5.50 and one free C _ k _ . Then a hamb _ _ ger and chips for $5.00, and then another fr _ _ Coke, thank you."

I thought that was a lot for a small boy who did not look even th _ _ t _ _ n years old, but I had to give it to him bec _ _ se he had _ _ dered it and I did not want to lose my job over this.

Back at the off _ _ _ Bob, anoth _ _ pizza man who d _ _ ls with the wa _ _ s, told me that a little boy of twelve had run aw _ _ from the local fost _ _ h _ m _ . He had taken an excessive am _ _ nt of money from the children and from the safe.

By now it was twelve at n _ _ _ t and I did not want to go back to the h _ _ se in the d _ _ k so I decided to go in the m _ _ ning.

I w_k_ up in the small h _ _ rs, still thinking about the b _ _ . I had a pic _ _ _ _ of him in my h _ _ d, all alone in the house. I l _ _ ked at my wa _ _ _ . It was two-th _ _ ty am. There were some ques_ _ _ _ s I wanted to ask and so I decided to ret _ _ n to the cott _ _ _ as s _ _ n as it got l _ _ _ t.

2. What do you think happened next? Use a mindmap to note your ideas and then write your own continuation of the story in your exercise book. Proofread your work, checking for spelling mistakes, punctuation, and use of paragraphs, as well as words left out or written in the wrong order.

Consonant digraph ph

Philip has a **ph**oto of So**ph**ie.

1. Auditory Introduction. (See page 13.)
2. Visual Introduction. (See page 13.)
4. Introduce the clueword and Spelling/Reading Cards.
3. Say **photo** f. Consonant digraph **ph** says f.

5. Highlight the **ph** and practice reading these words. When you are ready, read the words to your teacher.

phone	graph	phase	phrase	orphan
trophy	phonics	dolphin	gopher	phantom
photo	prophet	phony	elephant	pamphlet

6. Listen as your teacher gives you some words. (See page 15.) Write **ph** in the box if you hear f in the word.

1	2	3	4	5	6	7	8

More about consonant digraph ph

1. Find 15 of the words below in the Word Search. The words go down and across.

hyphen	lymph	sapphire	prophet
typhoon	phobia	epitaph	phosphate
phrase	pharmacy	autobiography	phial
sphinx	emphasis	hemisphere	telegraph
aphid	pheasant	amphibian	philosophy
physics	pamphlet	cacophony	graph

f	g	n	t	p	p	m	c	a	c	o	p	h	o	n	y	q
x	y	j	s	h	h	q	l	z	e	p	i	t	a	p	h	d
z	m	m	p	o	o	t	e	b	q	k	f	g	r	a	p	h
t	p	x	h	b	s	x	a	m	p	h	i	b	i	a	n	j
y	h	s	i	i	p	a	w	j	p	h	y	s	i	c	s	y
p	p	h	n	a	h	p	h	i	l	o	s	o	p	h	y	p
h	h	e	x	e	a	h	p	r	o	p	h	e	t	a	p	h
o	k	u	v	z	t	i	j	p	e	n	h	e	w	t	q	i
o	p	m	f	m	e	d	p	h	a	r	m	a	c	y	u	a
n	a	u	t	o	b	i	o	g	r	a	p	h	y	h	o	l

2. Write the words you have found in the Word Search. Look up any words you do not know in your dictionary. Write a brief definition in your exercise book for each of the words.

More about consonant digraph ph

1. Highlight the **ph** in these words. Your teacher will read the words to you. Write the number of syllables you hear in the box. Practice reading the words and then read them to your teacher.

hyphen	☐	aphid	☐	phrase	☐
typhoon	☐	pheasant	☐	prophet	☐
amphibian	☐	cacophony	☐	epitaph	☐
sapphire	☐	telegraph	☐	phial	☐
philosophy	☐	pharmacy	☐	pamphlet	☐
physics	☐	emphasis	☐	phobia	☐
phosphate	☐	hemisphere	☐	graph	☐
sphinx	☐	lymph	☐	autobiography	☐

2. Listen to the teacher. (See page 16.) Write the words you hear under these headings.

f **f**   ff **f**   ph **f**   gh **f**

_____   _____   _____   _____

_____   _____   _____   _____

More about consonant digraph ph

1. Listen as your teacher reads the words in the box. Fill in the blanks to complete each **ph** word next to its definition. Use the dictionary if you are unsure of a word.

radiography	p h _____	1. Ghost
sphere	_ p h ____	2. Globe
orphan	___ p h ___	3. Motherless and fatherless child
philanthropy	____ p h _____	4. Large land-based mammal
geography	_____ p h _____	5. Use for communication
biography	_____ p h _____	6. Air surrounding the planet
microphone	_____ p h _	7. Study of the world
elephant	_____ p h ___	8. Change of form, e.g., tadpole to frog
ephemeral	_____ p h _	9. Obtaining X-ray pictures
alphabet	_____ p h _	10. Study of the statistics of births, deaths, etc.
telephone	_____ p h _	11. Written account of person's life
decipher	_____ p h ____	12. Makes the voice louder
dolphin	_____ p h ___	13. Decode
phantom	___ p h ___	14. Friendly sea creature
demography	__ p h _____	15. All the letters
atmosphere	_ p h _____	16. Lasting only a short time
metamorphosis	p h _____	17. Love of humankind

More about consonant digraph ph

1. Fill in ph and read:

___ilip claimed his tro___y and then strode to the

micro___one he uttered a few ___rases of trium___ on

behalf of the team the atmos___ere was ___enomenal after-

wards he signed autogra___ books as the press took

___otogra___s next day the newspaper ran paragra___s on

this tele___one operator who once lived in an or___anage

but whose ___ysical strengths have made him a great foot-

ball star he plans to write his autobiogra___y

Now correct the punctuation and capitalization. You should find 6 sentences.
Ask your teacher to check your work then use the sentences for dictation in your
exercise book.

**How can you tell
if there's an elephant
in your oven?**

You can't get
the door shut.

Conjunctions
Words used to join simple sentences

| and | if | although | but | because | when | unless | so |

1. Use the words in the box above to join two simple sentences together to make one sentence that is more interesting. Each word may be used only once. Write the conjunction on the line and number the second part to match the first one. **Don't forget to change the punctuation!**

1. He ran to catch the bus. _____ ☐ She loved drinking milk.

2. You will cut your finger. _____ ☐ I had to change my clothes.

3. She enjoyed eating pancakes. _____ ☐ He was just too late.

4. I was caught in a storm. _____ ☐ You are not careful.

5. We shall not pass our exams. _____ ☐ He broke the rules.

6. He was severely punished. _____ ☐ We review carefully.

7. She was expected to work. _____ ☐ He saved the orphans.

8. He was rewarded for bravery. _____ ☐ She was only eight years old.

2. Conjunctions can be used at the beginning of the sentence. Note the need for a comma. Example: He had a cold. He still went to school...
  Although he had a cold, he still went to school.

Complete this exercise as you did in Section 1, but this time place the conjunction at the beginning of the sentence.

1. _____ He had eaten his meal. ☐ He will incur annoyance.

2. _____ She was awarded a grant. ☐ She had to take a taxi home.

3. _____ He changes his attitude. ☐ She still swam 20 laps a day.

4. _____ She was over eighty. ☐ He did the washing up.

5. _____ She had lost her keys. ☐ She will go to the university.

3. Listen to your teacher read 5 sentences from Sections 1 and 2. Write them in your exercise book.

More about conjunctions
Interesting sentences

1. Improve the passage, by adding suitable **conjunctions** from the list on page 95 to make more interesting sentences. Change the punctuation and capitalization as needed.

I once spent a wonderful day beside a rushing river in the North of Scotland. We picnicked on the short grass. We passed the time relaxing in the sunshine. We chose a spot near a waterfall. We wanted to watch the salmon leaping. The signal that it was time for some action came. We noticed a crowd starting to gather on the platform overhanging the waterfall. The water was crystal clear. We could observe the amazing creatures swimming purposefully upstream over the pebbles. Suddenly you would see a flash of wriggling silver as a female bravely flung herself up over the rapids. She dashed herself on the rocks as she fought the current. This did not deter her. Often she would be washed back down to start again. She landed just short of the pool above. Usually she would succeed. It might take several attempts. She may reach her spawning ground to lay her eggs at last. She is lured onto the end of a poacher's rod. I believe we can all learn something about courage and perseverance from a salmon.

(You should be able to add 8 **conjunctions,** removing 8 **periods.**)

2. Highlight the **adverbs** in the passage. You should find 4.

More about adverbs

1. Choose 3 appropriate **adverbs** from the box to add to each verb below.

swiftly	safely	skillfully	eventually	cunningly
easily	lazily	clumsily	intently	bravely
slowly	neatly	carefully	craftily	attentively

He swam _____ _____ _____

She landed _____ _____ _____

We watched _____ _____ _____

They succeeded _____ _____ _____

She is lured _____ _____ _____

2. Write 2 of your own sentences using **adverbs.**

1. _____

2. _____

Long vowel pattern ew

The cr**ew** hates st**ew**!

1. Auditory Introduction. (See page 13.)
2. Visual Introduction. (See page 13.)
3. Introduce the clueword and Spelling/Reading Cards.
4. Say st**ew** **U** and say cr**ew** **OO**. The pattern **ew** is the 1st spelling choice for the **U** or **OO** sound at the end of a word.

5. Highlight the **ew** and practice reading these words. When you are ready read the words to your teacher.

pew	stew	few	new	dew	slew
screw	crew	brew	knew	threw	cashew
drew	flew	grew	jewel	pewter	sewer
mildew	nephew		curfew	screwdriver	

6. Listen as your teacher gives you some words. (See page 16.) Write **ew** in the box if you hear **U** or **OO** in the word.

1	2	3	4	5	6	7	8

More about long vowel pattern <u>ew</u>

1. The letters **ew** together usually say **U**

   BUT when letters **j**, **r**, or **l**, come before the **ew** they say **OO**.

   (Remember: **J**une **r**ules **L**uke.)

2. Complete each word with an **ew**. Read the words to your teacher.

   d_____   f_____   n_____   h_____

   p_____   y_____   st_____   sp_____

   sk_____   vi_____   p_____ter   curf_____

   ren_____   mild_____   neph_____

3. Highlight **ew** and read the words to your teacher.

   blew   brew   crew   drew   flew   grew

   slew   Jews   jewel   Hebrew   cashew   chew

4. Complete these sentences with words from Sections 2 and 3.

   1. Many _____ live in Israel and speak _____.

   2. During a _____ everyone must return to their
      homes and be off the streets by a fixed time.

   3. We watched the _____ as it _____ across
      the marsh and landed in the shallow water.

5. Listen to the teacher. (See page 16.) Write the headings "st**ew** **U**" and
   "cr**ew** **OO**" in your exercise book. Listen carefully to each word and write
   the word in the correct column.

The hostess had prepared a superb lunch for the crew. The food was displayed on long trestle tables under the huge yew trees on the grounds of her stately home. The crew members were on leave for two weeks from their frigate in the North Sea. It was a new naval vessel, The H.M.S. Voyager, and they were very proud of their record.

1

When the waiters announced that the meal was served, the guests formed a hungry line beside the flower beds, waiting to help themselves to the tasty dishes.

2

The variety was incredible. There were prawn cocktails; platters of exotic cold meats; bubbling bowls of spicy stews and curries with thick creamy sauces; salads garnished with cashew nuts and vegetables of every description. The desserts were displayed on a separate table to be investigated later.

3

Andrew's mouth watered as he helped himself to a huge portion of stew. He found an empty chair, placed his paper napkin in his lap, and prepared to enjoy his meal. To his great surprise, the meat was very hard to chew. Just as he was wondering what to do with a large piece of sinew in his mouth, the captain's daughter came over to join him and he had to swallow the meat whole in order not to appear too rude.

4

More about ew

1. Copy the following sentence twice on the lines below. Check the one you prefer.

"Phew," gasped my nephew, Andrew, as he drew
a deep breath and blew up the last balloon.

2. Look up the definitions of these words in your dictionary. Write each word and its meaning in your exercise book.

trestle	frigate	vessel
sinew	portion	garnish

3. Write a synonym and an antonym for each of these words:

proud	spicy	swallow
exotic	secretly	feed

How did Newton discover gravity?   By sheer apple – ication.

U	
ew
stew

oo
ew
crew

Do you know these math words?

I. Match the words in the box to the diagrams and definitions.

acute angle	denominator	kilometer	radius
area	diameter	millimeter	ratio
average	equation	numerator	right angle
circumference	equilateral triangle	obtuse angle	scalene triangle
co-ordinates	graph	perimeter	square number
compasses	hypotenuse	perpendicular	sum
consecutive numbers	integers	product	
degree	isosceles triangle	protractor	

Pair of numbers that plot a position   c _____

o _____   Angle of less than 180° and more than 90°

Extent of a surface   a _____

c _____   "Next door" numbers, e.g., 23, 24, 25

Distance around a shape or object   p _____

d _____   Unit of measurement for angles

Diagram of relationship between 2 variables   g _____

k _____   A measure of length (1000 m)

Piece of equipment for drawing circles   c _____

n _____   Number above the line in a fraction

Straight line through the centre of a circle   d _____

r _____   An angle of 90°

Triangle with 3 equal sides and 3 equal angles   e _____

p _____   When 2 numbers are multiplied together, e.g., 2 x 2 the answer is the

Math words, continued

Add a list of numbers and divide the total by the amount of numbers to get the   a _____

$$\begin{array}{r} 5 \\ 2 \\ 4 \\ \underline{1} + \\ 12 \div 4 = 3 \end{array}$$

$\dfrac{4}{9}$ ←   d _____   Number below the line in a fraction

Longest side of a right angled triangle, opposite the right angle.   h _____

a _____   Angle measuring less than 90¡

Triangle with 2 equal sides and 2 equal angles   i _____

r _____   Related in size or amount, proportionately

Positive and negative whole numbers including 0   i _____

0 5 -99

1cm = 10?   m _____   A measure of length 1cm = 10?   m

Number made by multiplying another number by itself, e.g., 2 x 2 = 4, 3 x 3 = 9   s _____

3 x 3 = 9

r _____   Distance from the centre of a circle to the circumference

Used for measuring angles   p _____

p _____   At right angles

The perimeter of a circle   c _____

s _____   A triangle with no equal sides

Mathematical statement that 2 things are equal   e _____

2x+3y = a

---

2. Listen to your teacher. (See page 16.) Test yourself. Write the answers in your exercise book to the questions you hear. Try not to look at this page, but use it to check your answers.

---

3. Listen to your teacher. (See page 16.) Solve the puzzle by answering each question "yes" or "no" and writing the appropriate letter in the box.

I. Y   N   **2.** Y   N   **3.** Y   N   **4.** Y   N   **5.** Y   N   **6.** Y   N

| P | R | | A | T | | D | B | | S | I | | C | U | | S | E |

| | | | | | | | |

Vowel digraph pattern aw

A h**aw**k's **aw**ful cl**aw**s can dr**aw** blood.

1. Auditory Introduction. (See page 13.)
2. Visual Introduction. (See page 13.)
3. Introduce the clueword and Spelling/Reading Cards.
4. Say cl**aw** **aw**. The sound is the same as **sauce** **aw**.

5. Highlight the **aw** and practice reading these words. When you are ready, read the words to your teacher.

law	jaw	claw	raw	paw	thaw
straw	shawl	yawn	crawl	brawl	squaw
lawn	awning	squawk	fawn	draw	drawl
straw	awful	saw	flaw	sprawl	pawn

6. Listen as your teacher gives you some words. (See page 16.) Write **aw** in the box if you hear **aw** in the word.

1	2	3	4	5	6	7	8

More about vowel digraph pattern aw

1. Listen as your teacher gives you some words. (See page 16.)
   Check the word you hear.

cow	caw	saw	sow	drawn	drown	raw	row	owning	awning
☐	☐	☐	☐	☐	☐	☐	☐	☐	☐
bowl	bawl	dawn	down	awe	owe	law	low	brown	brawn
☐	☐	☐	☐	☐	☐	☐	☐	☐	☐

2. Read these words to your teacher.

withdrawn   unlawful

lawn mower   trawler

strawberry   hawthorn

dawdle   sprawling

crawling   pawn

sawdust   pawpaw

awkward   squawk

coleslaw

3. Read
   1. Raw prawns should be boiled before eating.
   2. The tawny owl swooped swiftly and caught the mouse with its claws.
   3. The brawny lads got into another brawl.
   4. He scrawled his name on the picture he had drawn.

More about vowel digraph pattern aw

1. Choose from the words in section 2, page 106 to answer the clues and fill in the grid.

   1. Fishing vessel

   2. Extremely quiet and reserved

   3. Feeling embarrassed or clumsy

   4. Tropical fruit

   5. Moving slowly on all fours

   6. Cuts the grass

   7. Cabbage salad

   8. Against the law

   9. Bush or tree which flowers in May

   10. Red summer fruit

   11. Shavings from chopped wood

   12. Lying with legs and arms flung out

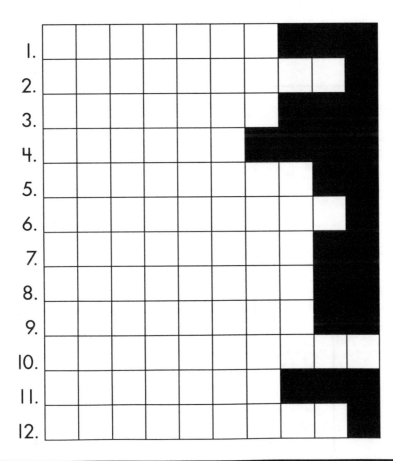

More about vowel digraph pattern aw

1. Pretend you are married with children and complete the family tree choosing words from the box.   **m** = married   ♂ = male   ♀ = female

mother	son	daughter	grandmother	uncle
son-in-law	father	sister	granddaughter	aunt
father-in-law	mother-in-law		grandson	brother
nephew	daughter-in-law	niece		brother-in-law
	grandfather	sister-in-law		

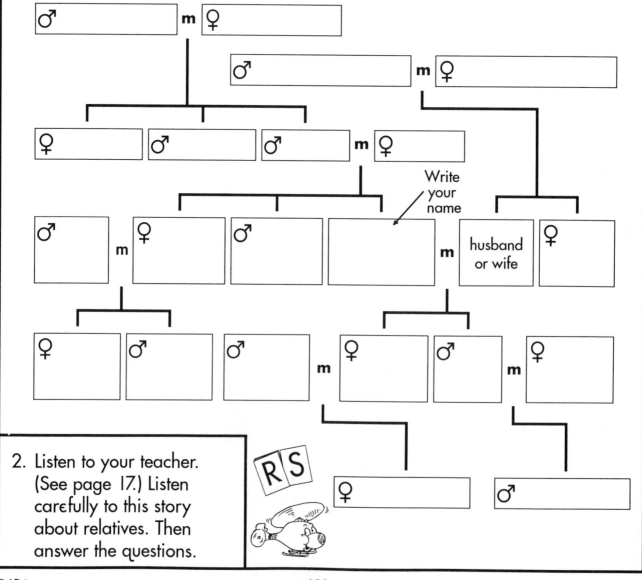

2. Listen to your teacher. (See page 17.) Listen carefully to this story about relatives. Then answer the questions.

Vowel digraph choices aw au ow ou

1. Underline or highlight **aw** in each word. Circle the word in each line that does not contain **aw**. Read all the words. The first one has been done for you.

cl<u>aw</u>	j<u>aw</u>	(cow)	dr<u>aw</u>
dawn	clown	yawn	lawn
shawl	trawl	owl	crawl

thaw	law	paw	low
draw	straw	flow	flaw
drawl	bowl	brawl	sprawl

Underline or highlight **au** in each word. Circle the word in each line that does not contain **au**. Read all the words.

pause	cause	blouse	clause
tout	daub	taut	gauze
fauna	trauma	aura	rouse

haunt	count	gaunt	taunt
haul	maul	foul	fault
paunch	pouch	launch	staunch

2. Listen to your teacher. (See page 17.) Listen to the words and write them in the correct columns.

Nouns	Adjectives
audience	audible

More vowel digraph choices aw au ow ou

1. Listen to the teacher and complete the following sentences. (See page 17.)

   1. He insists he _____ a flying _____ last _____ night.

   2. The Japanese love _____ squid dipped in horse-radish _____.

   3. No one _____ what _____ _____ to become extinct.

   4. The _____ coming from _____ car is against the _____.

   5. The _____ attended the _____ of his latest book and agreed to sign copies of the first edition for the _____.

   6. I love _____ but I have never tasted mango or _____.

   7. The children _____ the _____ when fishing in the river.

   8. _____ is a disease of the liver and _____ _____ of the skin.

   9. _____ went to _____ for a part in the pantomime.

   10. A lovely _____ _____ covered her _____ shoulders.

2. Ask your teacher for a a spelling test. (See page 18.) Listen for every sound and write the words in your exercise book.

Sound Pictures ——→ Words

Make the Sound Pictures, write the words.

Look Say	Listen Name the letters	Write
Example: **k er l d**	\ \ \ \ / / / – c-u-r-l-e-d – / / \ \ \	*curled*
1. **p er p'l**		1. _____
2. **v oy i j**		2. _____
3. **n oy z**		3. _____
4. **v oy s**		4. _____
5. **n E s**		5. _____
6. **t I**		6. _____
7. **aw t i s t i k**		7. _____
8. **tr aw m a t i k**		8. _____
9. **s kw aw k**		9. _____
10. **aw f oo l**		10. _____
11. **n e f U**		11. _____
12. **k er f U**		12. _____

Syllable pattern -sion

An angry proces**sion** is on the televi**sion**!

1. Auditory Introduction. (See page 13.)
2. Visual Introduction. (See page 13.)
3. Introduce the clueword and Reading/Spelling Cards.
4. Say **procession** `sh'n`. Say **television** `zh'n`. Syllable pattern tion is found at the end of a word.

5. Highlight the **sion** and practice reading these words. When you are ready, read the words to your teacher.

mansion	pension	passion	tension
commission	extension	suspension	transmission
convulsion	confession	admission	suppression

What sound did the **sion** have in the above words?_____

6. Highlight the **sion** and practice reading these words. When you are ready, read the words to your teacher.

adhesion	version	conclusion	division
profusion	illusion	occasion	revision

What sound did the **sion** have in the above words?_____

More about syllable pattern -sion

1. You have now learned two ways to spell the **s h' n** sound.

   frac**tion** **s h' n**   proces**sion** **s h' n**.

2. How do you know which to use?

   1. Use **-tion** after a short **i** sound, a long vowel sound, and most consonants.

   2. Use **-sion** <u>always</u> when it follows consonants **s** and **l**.

   Use **-sion** <u>some of the time</u> when it follows consonant **n**.

3. All the words below have consonant **n** before the **s h' n** sound. Put an "x" on the line if the word doesn't end in -**sion**. Practice reading and when you are ready, read to your teacher.

   mention ____   dimension ____

   expansion ____   prevention ____

   detention ____   indention ____

   pension ____   mansion ____

   attention ____   contention ____

   intervention ____   retention ____

   convention ____   intention ____

   invention ____   extension ____

   dissension ____   suspension ____

4. Your teacher will give you some of the above words above for spelling. Write them in your exercise book.

More about syllable pattern -sion

sion is never found at the beginning of a word.

1.   After the letters **l**, **n**, and **s**, **sh'n** is usually spelled **sion**.

Here is a mnemonic to help you remember this.
LIONS **N**EED **S**OCKS.
Can you think of a better one?

_____
_____
_____
_____
_____
_____
_____

2. The **sh'n** sound is ALWAYS SPELLED -**sion**. Write the words:

     e ks t e n sh'n   **k o n v u l sh'n**

     _____   _____

  t e l e v i zh'n   **i n v A zh'n**   **e ks p l O zh'n**

  _____   _____   _____

3. Copy the sentence twice in your exercise book. Check the one you like best.

Division and indecision in political parties cause disillusionment.

More about -tion and -sion

1. Listen to your teacher. (See page 18.) Write each word you hear in the correct column.

s h'n -sion	s h'n -tion
_____	_____
_____	_____
_____	_____
_____	_____
_____	_____

2. Now write a good synonym for each word that you have written in section 1, next to the word, on the line provided. Use your thesaurus to help you.

3. Who will take the wise decision

   To abolish long division,

   Never use this senseless punishment again.

   Please let future generations

   With much better calculations,

   Put an end to all this agony and pain.

How many syllables can you count in each line?
Can you work out the syllable and rhyme pattern in the verse?
Now write a similar silly verse of your own in your exercise book.

More about syllable pattern -tion and -sion

1. Punctuate this passage.

the collision happened at the
corner of station road and
coronation drive this was not
usually an accident black spot
but roadwork had caused a
diversion matthew conroys
vision of the alternative route
signs had been temporarily
blocked by a stationary coach
as he was craning his neck to

check the directions he lost control of the rolls royce there was no
doubt that he had been approaching the junction too quickly the
sickening crunching noise confirmed his worst fears and the next
thing he remembered was waking up in an ambulance on the way
to his admission to the local hospital a few hours later after a blood
transfusion some stitches and some attention to a few minor abra-
sions the nurse confirmed that he was only suffering from mild con-
cussion he could probably expect to be discharged in the morning
gradually it dawned on him that his decision to take the chiefs pride
and joy for a spin had been catastrophic

You should have made 9 sentences using 9 **periods**, 6 **commas**, and
2 **apostrophes** and you should have added 16 **capital letters**.

2. Dictation. Your teacher will read you the last 5 sentences from the story for
dictation. Write them in your exercise book.

Test your reading skills
Beat the clock.

1. Time yourself reading the word wall. Record your time and then try to beat it. Aim for 2 minutes.

curtail 1	spoiled 2	brief 3	alloy 4
untie 5	chariot 6	unemployment 7	gauze 8
crawl 9	pheasant 10	plied 11	disturbing 12
squirt 13	creative 14	fuel 15	destroy 16
magpie 17	dueling 18	Polaroid 19	shriek 20	faultless 21
diabetic 22	fraud 23	circumstances 24	lawyer 25
diesel 26	biological 27	inaudible 28	geography 29
automatic 30	microphone 31	desert 32	environment 33
authority 34	physics 35	radiography 36	trawler 37
client 38	furlong 39	awkward 40	choice 41	audio 42
turquoise 43	thieves 44	authenticity 45	mischief 46
reprographic 47	disappointment 48	unavoidable 49	grief 50
lawn mower 51	reproduction 52	precision 53	satisfaction 54

2. Work out the percentage of words you are able to read in one minute. If you can read all of the words in one minute that is 100%. Half of the words = 50%. Ask your teacher if you need help to work this out.

Long vowel pattern ue

Don't arg**ue** over the gl**ue**!

1. Auditory Introduction. (See page 13.)
2. Visual Introduction. (See page 13.)
3. Introduce the clueword and Reading/Spelling Cards.
4. Say **argue** **U** and **glue** **OO**. The pattern **ue** is the 2nd spelling choice for the **U** or **OO** sound at the end of a word.

5. Highlight the **ue** and practice reading these words. When you are ready, read the words to your teacher.

glue	clue	sue	due	true	hue
rescue	endue	virtue	pursue	value	blue
continue	avenue	revenue	barbecue		

6. Listen as your teacher gives you some words. (See page 18.) Write **ue** in the box if you hear **U** or **OO** at the end of the word.

1	2	3	4	5	6	7	8

More long vowel pattern ue

1. Read.

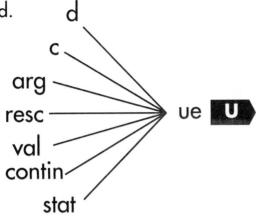

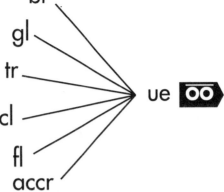

---

2. Notice that just as with the **ew** words, when the letters **r** or **l** come before **ue**, **ue** makes the 👀 sound. Long **U**, no matter how it is spelled, can change to 👀 after the letters **j**, **r** and **l**.

---

3. Read and then fill in **U** or 👀 in the Sound Pictures.

mule ⬡   tube ⬡   rule ⬡   flute ⬡   duke ⬡   June ⬡

chew ⬡   yew ⬡   drew ⬡   skew ⬡   flew ⬡   Jew ⬡

hue ⬡   argue ⬡   blue ⬡   true ⬡   due ⬡   clue ⬡

---

4. Copy the following sentences twice. Check the one you like best.

We must continue to rescue endangered species.

They are invaluable.

More long vowel pattern ue

1. Syllable division. Remember the RULES!

   vccv   words split **vc/cv**
   vcv   words split **v/cv** (first choice)
   vcv   words split **vc/v** (second choice)

   Mark the **vc** pattern and split:

   argue   statue   value   rescue   venue   continue

   What did you notice about all the vcv words above?
   Did they split v/cv or vc/v?

2. Use your dictionary to find the meanings of these words and use each one in an interesting sentence:

   accrue _____

   _____

   venue _____

   _____

   revenue _____

   _____

   retinue _____

   _____

   residue _____

   _____

   pursue _____

   _____

More long vowel pattern ue

1. Read the word and choose its 3 synonyms from the box below.

true = accurate, authentic, correct

accrue = _____, _____, _____

venue = _____, _____, _____

revenue= _____, _____, _____

retinue = _____, _____, _____

residue = _____, _____, _____

location	income	attendants	followers	accumulate
place	escort	deposit	profits	whereabouts
amass	yield	dregs	collect	sediment

2. Use the words in Section 1 above to complete these sentences.

1. What is the true _____ of that _____?

2. Despite the weather, emergency _____teams
   _____with their fight to save the crew of the
   rapidly submerging tanker.

3. Why must we always _____over whose house will be
   the _____for the party?

Why are cooks so cruel?

Because they beat the eggs and whip the cream.

Silent letters and strange letter patterns

1. A **silent** letter is one which you need to spell a word, but which is **not sounded** when you read or say the word.

   Match the following words with their pictures, underlining the silent letters:

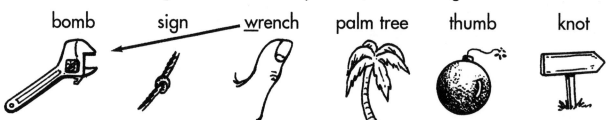

   bomb   sign   <u>w</u>rench   palm tree   thumb   knot

2. Underline the **silent** letter in each word. Write the silent letter in the brackets at the end of each line:

   lamb   tomb   limb   numb   [   ]

   crumb   dumb   plumber   comb   [   ]

   knob   kneel   knock   knocker   knocking   knee   [   ]

   knit   knew   knight   know   knowledge   knelt   [   ]

   calf   half   talk   walk   stalk   folk   [   ]

   gnat   gnu   gnash   sign   signing   [   ]

   resign   signed   ensign   campaign   [   ]

   wrote   written   wreck   wrap   wriggle   [   ]

   writhe   wrong   wring   wreath   Wainwright   [   ]

1. Listen to your teacher. (See page 18.) Add the correct words to these sentences:

   1. We went _____ because we did not follow all the _____ as we went on a walk.

   2. The _____ festival was a great success. The weather was mild and _____ so that we did not need to _____ up to keep warm.

   3. The _____ _____ were _____ loudly as he squared up to his opponent at the jousting contest. They clashed so violently, they had to be _____ apart.

   4. I felt _____ as we _____ down and _____ the _____ of the _____ mummy in the _____.

2. 4 fun joke

   Will you remember me in a month? Of course.

   Will you remember me in a year? Certainly.

   Will you remember me in two years? Yes.

   Will you remember me in three years? Of course.

   Knock, knock. Who's there?

   See, you've forgotten me already.

3. See if you can make up a limerick, or some jokes, using any of the silent letter words in Section 2 on page 122.

Vowel suffix -ous

Snakes alive! Danger**ous**, venom**ous** ones!

1. Auditory Introduction. (See page 13.)
2. Visual Introduction. (See page 13.)
3. Introduce the clueword and Spelling/Reading Cards.
4. Say **dangerous** **U** **S**. -**ous** is a vowel suffix which is added to a noun to make an adjective meaning "full of." Example: That quarry is a **danger** (noun) to children. It is a **dangerous** (adjective) quarry.

5. Highlight the -**ous** and practice reading these words. When you are ready, read the words to your teacher.

serious	various	nervous	fabulous	famous
generous	jealous		numerous	humorous
pompous	continuous	prosperous		marvelous

6. Listen as your teacher gives you some words. (See page 18.) Write **ous** in the box if you hear **U** **S** in the word.

1	2	3	4	5	6	7	8

More about vowel suffix -ous

1. Listen to the teacher. (See page 18.) Write a number 1 in the box of the 1st word you hear, a 2 in the box of the second word and so on.

generous ☐   famous ☐   venomous ☐

ridiculous ☐   marvelous ☐   tremendous ☐

jealous ☐   poisonous ☐   adventurous ☐

treacherous ☐

2. Trace filling in **ous**

pomp_____   fabul_____   poison_____

venom_____   vari_____   nerv_____

3. Write at least one **-ous** word in each sentence from Sections 2 or 3 above. Complete the sentences in your exercise book, using your own interesting ideas.

   1. Which are the most _____ quicksands or avalanches?

   2. There in the undergrowth lurked a _____ snake.

   3. He looked utterly _____ in his fancy dress costume which consisted of ...

   4. The elephant looked _____ when compared with ...

   5. He had a _____ benefactor who gave him a grant to start ...

   6. It was a _____ idea to ...

   7. Football players, basketball players and . . . . . . have all become more _____ since the advent of television.

4. Which two **-ous** words in Section 1 are synonyms? Write them below.

_____   _____

More about vowel suffix -ous

1. A few adjectives end in **-eous**. Try reading these words.

hideous   spontaneous   erroneous   simultaneous

miscellaneous   courteous   instantaneous

Listen to the teacher to check that you were right.

How many words can you make from the letters in **instantaneous**?

_____ _____ _____

_____ _____ _____

_____ _____ _____

_____ _____ _____

_____ _____ _____

_____ _____ _____

_____ _____ _____

2. Match these words with their meanings:

spontaneous	an assortment
simultaneous	monstrous
courteous	mistaken
instantaneous	unplanned
erroneous	at once
hideous	at the same time
miscellaneous	polite

3. A few words are spelled with **-uous**. Explain what they mean below:

sumptuous _____

contemptuous _____

More about vowel suffix -ous

1. Look in the newspaper and see if you can find three **-ous** words and three **-eous** words.

2. When a **noun** ends in the ⬢U⬢S sound it is spelled **us**.

crocus	bonus	virus	citrus	octopus
Pegasus	Fergus	discuss	exodus	chorus
genius	sinus	bogus	cactus	campus
focus	Venus	cenous	octopus	hippopotamus

3. Listen to the teacher. (See page 18.) Write the words you hear under the correct headings.

-ous _____ _____ _____

-eous _____ _____ _____

-uous _____ _____ _____

-us _____ _____ _____

Baby snake:
Mum, are we
poisonous snakes?

Mother snake:
No, why?

Baby snake:
Good, because I
just bit my lip.

R S

Consonant digraph ch

The **ch**emist has a cure for stoma**chach**e.

1. Auditory Introduction. (See page 13.)
2. Visual Introduction. (See page 13.)
3. Introduce the clueword and Spelling/Reading Cards.
4. Say **chemist** **k**.

5. Highlight the **ch** and practice reading these words. When you are ready, read the words to your teacher.

echo	chord	school	chorus
ache	chrome	Christmas	schedule
orchestra	chronic	scheme	monarch
orchid		anchor	

6. Listen as your teacher gives you some words. (See page 18.) Write **ch** in the box if you hear **k** in the word.

1	2	3	4	5	6	7	8

More about digraph ch

1. Underline the **ch** in each word. Write **k** above each **ch**.

or<u>ch</u>id   charisma   chronic

chaos   cholera   echo

character   bronchitis   chronicle

chord   lichen   chlorine

melancholy   chasm   mechanic

Divide the words into syllables and read them to your teacher.

2. Underline or highlight each **ch k** in the passage below. You should find 10. Read the passage aloud.

The schooner slipped anchor and slid smoothly past the dusty wharves with their crumbling architecture and on towards the open sea.

Despite his charisma, a carefully planned scheme to restore the exiled monarch had failed once again, and there was a strong sense of melancholy aboard the boat as she sailed out towards a setting sun. A final blast from the ship's horn echoed around the channel as this noble character stood at the stern regarding for the last time his small country which was now on the brink of chaos.

More about digraph ch

1. Read these words. Match them to the clues to complete the puzzle.

chlorophyll   cholesterol   chrysalis   chromosome   chronological

1. Events arranged in order of their occurrence.
2. Structure in cell which carries genetic information.
3. Green pigment in plants responsible for light absorption for photosynthesis.
4. Too much in the blood supply can lead to heart disease.
5. Caterpillar's form while changing into a butterfly or moth.

Consonant digraph ch

The **ch**ef sips **ch**ampagne.

1. Auditory Introduction. (See page 13.)
2. Visual Introduction. (See page 13.)
3. Introduce the clueword and Spelling/Reading Cards.
4. Say **chef** **s h**.

5. Highlight the **ch** in each sentence. Write **s h** above each **ch** and then read the words to your teacher.

chivalry	machine	brochure	chauffeur
chalet	avalanche	moustache	chute
parachute	chiffon	chevron	chicanery
Chicago	chaise	chandelier	eustachian

6. Listen as your teacher gives you some words. (See page 18.) Write **ch** in the box if you hear **s h** in the word.

1	2	3	4	5	6	7	8	9	10

More about consonant digraph ch

1. Read the words in the boxes and use them to complete the sentences.

ch **k**	ch **s h**	ch **c h**
Christmas orchestra	chalets	choosing checking
choir architect	chauvinists brochure	avalanche challenge
technical school	parachuting Charlotte	

1. The _____ and _____ were _____ carols for the _____ concert.

2. The ski holiday _____ did not mention that the _____ were close to the site of last year's _____.

3. The _____ was _____ his _____ drawings for the new _____.

4. _____ found herself amongst a group of male _____ when she took up the _____ of _____ as a hobby.

2. Listen to your teacher. Use the above sentences for dictation. Write them in your exercise book.

3. Listen to your teacher. (See page 19.) Write each word you hear in the correct column.

ch **k**	ch **s h**	ch **c h**
_____	_____	_____
_____	_____	_____
_____	_____	_____

What's the difference between a wet day and a lion with toothache?

One pours with rain and the other roars with pain.

Introducing -que
Spelling choices for **k** c ch ck k and -que

1. A few words end in **-que** **k**. Fill in the sound picture and read these words.

antique   technique   plaque

unique   oblique   grotesque

2. Fill in **c**, **k**, **-ck**, **ch**, or **-que** **k** as the correct spelling choice.

___ingdom	qui___ly	wal___ed	___onversation
e___o	uni___	___urlew	me___ani___
ba___teria	tragi___	dar___ness	heada___e
snoo___er	haddo___	in___lusion	___ri___et

3. Fill in the correct spellings for the **k** sound in the following passage.

A uni____ feature of early Gree__ ar___ite__ture is the Dori___ __olumn. Its simple yet sturdy design so impressed the Vi__torian ar___ite__ts that they often __opied this __lassi__al style with the result that many of our great houses, s__ools and publi___ buildings e___o the tradition of the Parthenon in Athens.

Of __ourse some of the most impressive edifices on earth were __onstru__ted in the name of the world's most powerful religions. The early __athedrals of ___ristendom, the mos____s of Islam, and the Hindu or Buddhist temples of the Far East are testament to this fa__t.

Less pi__tures____ are the __ontemporary s__ys__rapers of New Yor__ , Singapore, and Hong __ong. Although they are all __onsiderable te___nologi__al achievements, these monuments to international business __orporations are sometimes grotes____ in appearance and la___ the grace and dignity of the __olonial period.

Now read the passage again and underline the key or topic sentence in each paragraph. The topic sentence is often the first sentence. It carries the main point of information.

Handwriting Practice
Trace and copy.

ou   authority

Their gaunt faces caused the launch of an appeal.

ph   photograph

His photograph of pheasants won the trophy.

ew   nephew

The curlew flew to join a few flamingoes.

aw   trawler

The hawk squawks as it launches its attack.

sion   tension   confusion

The extra dimension is an optical illusion.

ue   true   continue

We need valuable exports to accrue revenue.

I swear that spears will bring a dearth of birds.

Syllable pattern -cian

This pattern is never found at the beginning of a word.

1. Say **magician** s h'n .

Addition for magi**cian**s!

2. Highlight **cian** and read these words.

magician	obstetrician	optician	beautician	politician
technician	physician	electrician	dietician	mathematician

3. **cian** at the end of a word means: *A person who . . .*

Example: A person who plays a musical instrument is a musi**cian**.

4. Answer this riddle: What am I?

_ _ _ _ _ _ _ _ _

My first is in mouse but not the word house.

My second is in saddle not bottle or puddle.

My third is in golf, in garbage, and goat.

My fourth begins ice and invoice, not oat.

My fifth is in cushion and curlew and cat.

My sixth is the vowel in hit, wit not hat.

My seventh the vowel that is first of the bunch.

My last is in nice, in nonsense, and lunch.

Syllable pattern -cian

1. Write a *good* sentence to show the meaning of each of the words below.

Example:

The magician performed an amazing trick which had us all baffled. (Good.)

We all went to see the magician. (Not good. The word "magician" could be replaced by horse, baby, dentist etc.)

1. technician _____

   _____

2. physician _____

   _____

3. optician _____

   _____

4. electrician _____

   _____

5. beautician _____

   _____

6. dietician _____

   _____

7. politician _____

   _____

8. mathematician _____

   _____

More about syllable pattern -cian

1. Decode the Sound Pictures to complete the passage and then record it on tape.

Saturday was the day of the annual street carnival **pr O s e sh'n**.

Each year the committee chose a different cause to support. On this

O k A zh'n the **k o l e k sh'n** was in aid of "Rescue the

Earth." The excitement had been growing as everyone made their

pr e p ə r A sh'n z. Much **i m ə j i n A sh'n**

and skill had been used to create costumes that were even more dazzlingly

magnificent than last year's. The **m U z i sh'n z** had been practicing

and the **e l e k tr i sh'n z** had completed the

k o n e k sh'n z of microphones, loudspeakers, and electronic

synthesizers.

Imagine their **d e s p ə r A sh'n** when the parade was cancelled

by the **p o l i t i sh'n z** because of a threat by a fringe element of

rabble-rousers who were determined to cause chaos, promote **t e n sh'n**

and **k o n f U zh'n**, and disturb law and order.

2. In what tense is the passage written? Record the passage again, this time reading it in the present tense. Start with "Today."

3. Spell the words from the Sound Pictures in the passage above and write each word in the correct column in your exercise book. The number of words in each column is written in parentheses.

   sh'n -tion (5)   **sh'n** -sion (2)   **sh'n** -cian (3)   **zh'n** -sion (2)

Key points
Highlighting and reviewing the key points in a passage

1. Read. Then follow the directions found on the bottom of page 139.

Television... to watch or not to watch, that is the question.

Statisticians will tell you that the average teenager spends at least 30 hours per week watching television. As well as the facility of satellite channels, plans are afoot to extend the range of technology which will increase the number of programs which vie for our attention and viewing time. Add to this the further hours spent watching rented videos and one cannot help wondering what effect this might have on future generations.

There is no doubt that much of what we see on our screens is educational and provides entertainment and enjoyment. Documentaries; news broadcasts; sports; nature and wildlife programs from various regions of the earth; autobiographies; good literature and dramatic productions; children's and adults' quiz shows; and expertise shared by excellent chefs and other experts all help to extend knowledge.

By contrast, some of the soaps and movies can hardly be described as morally uplifting and may justifiably be judged as stirring up violence. Advertising could be seen as exploiting gullible young minds which are plied with so-called essential purchases.

If a whole day out of each week is spent in front of the television, one could argue that this may be contributing to the growing number of "couch potatoes" in our society, whose weight problems and physical fitness levels are rapidly becoming a cause for concern.

2. Using a highlighter pen, highlight the key (most important) words in the passage. Discuss them with your teacher and make sure you have collected all the important information.

3. Do you agree with the views expressed in the passage? Explain why or why not.

4. Have a debate with a friend. One of you must agree with the views expressed in the passage and the other must disagree with them.

Making a mindmap

1. Complete the mindmap by spraying out your ideas on the lines provided.
   Use drawings and colors to make it more interesting.

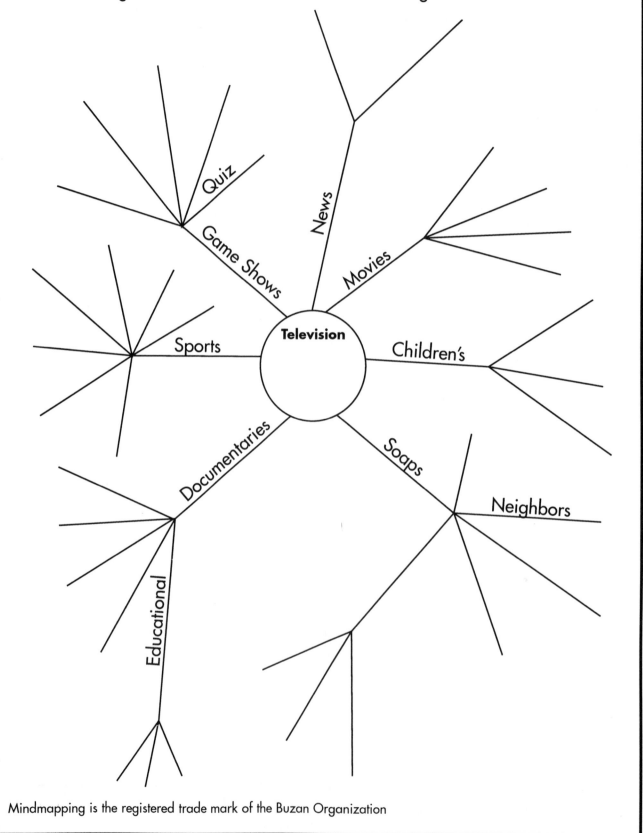

Mindmapping is the registered trade mark of the Buzan Organization

Learn to spell these tricky words

Work across ⟶

Read	Read	Trace, naming letters	Write
1. purpose	purpose	purpose	
2. scissors	scissors	scissors	
3. business	business	business	
4. possess	possess	possess	
5. success	success	success	
6. accident	accident	accident	
7. library	library	library	
8. accommodation	accommodation	accommodation	
9. language	language	language	

Learn to spell these tricky words, cont.

Work across ⟶

	Read	Read	Trace, naming letters	Write
1.	bicycle	bicycle	bicycle	
2.	certificate	certificate	certificate	
3.	genuine	genuine	genuine	
4.	decision	decision	decision	
5.	special	special	special	
6.	separate	separate	separate	
7.	vehicle	vehicle	vehicle	
8.	valuable	valuable	valuable	
9.	frequent	frequent	frequent	

fold

Hints on remembering and learning

1. **If you have a good auditory memory** using the tape recorder may help. Listening to your own recording of written material may be easier than reading it. Make up stories like the one your teacher will read to you.

   If you have a good visual memory make use of drawings, diagrams, and mindmaps. Use color. Actually, putting a mindmap together can be a good method of review and the result may be easier to memorize. (See page 140.)

2. Listen as your teacher reads a story (See page 19.). Your teacher may wish to record the story on a cassette tape. See if you can remember the content.

3. **Comparison of plant and animal cells.**

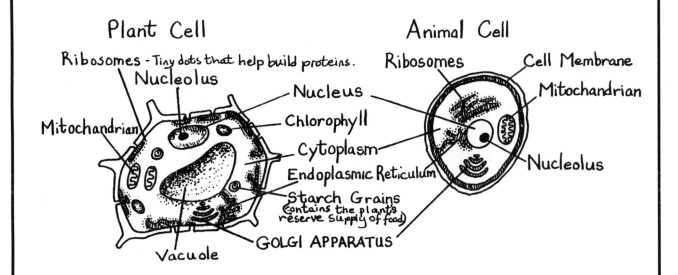

Plant Cell

Ribosomes - Tiny dots that help build proteins.
Nucleolus
Nucleus
Chlorophyll
Mitochandrian
Cytoplasm
Endoplasmic Reticulum
Starch Grains
(Contains the plants reserve supply of food)
GOLGI APPARATUS
Vacuole

Animal Cell

Ribosomes
Cell Membrane
Mitochandrian
Nucleolus

4. **Mnemonics:** Make up your own for sentences like the example for the 7 characteristics of life. Write them in your exercise book.

Example:

Sensitivity	**G**rowth	**R**espiration	**R**eproduction	**M**ovement	**E**xcretion	**N**utrition
Some	**G**irls	**R**ead	**R**ubbish	**M**agazines	**E**very	**N**ight.

Review planning

Where to study

1. Always study in the same place.
2. Find somewhere warm, well-ventilated, and with good lighting.
3. Keep this place quiet and free from distractions.
4. Make sure that you have a suitable desk and chair and all you need in the way of pencils, paper, and books. A tape recorder can be useful.

When to study

1. Find out if you study better in the morning or the evening.
2. Plan the week's study ahead and try to plan a study session for each day.
3. Plan recreation and relaxation as well!
4. Study sessions need to be from 1 – 3 hours long.
5. Remember you can only concentrate effectively for about 40 – 45 minutes, so build in learning breaks at the end of each period. Get up and do something completely different for 10 minutes or so.

How to study

1. Make sure there are no distractions such as noise, hunger, or cold.
2. List or schedule other things you have to do and get them off your mind.
3. Suppress any distracting and unwanted thoughts.
4. Take an interest in and make sure you understand what you are studying.
5. Have clear aims for each session and check your progress.

Why study?

Keep your aim in mind. Why do you want to pass these exams?
Which ones must you pass?

More review planning

Use this timetable to schedule your study sessions.

	Monday	Tuesday	Wednesday	Thursday	Friday	Saturday	Sunday
9-10 am							
10-11 am							
11-12 pm							
12-1 pm							
1-2 pm							
2-3 pm							
3-4 pm							
4-5 mp							
5-6 pm							
6-7 pm							
7-8 pm							
8-9 pm							
9-10 pm							

Some hints on remembering and learning

1. Never try to memorize what you don't understand.

2. Select important topics to learn. Don't waste valuable time on less important items. Ask your teacher which are the most important points and make a list of topics to learn.

3. Organize your notes into a logical sequence. Break up long pieces of information into manageable chunks. Use headings, highlighter pens, or colored paper to divide different topics.

4. Start each study session with a review of the last session. Go over notes or reading within 12 hours of previous session.

5. Make sure you have mastered each topic before leaving it for the next. Overlearn – go over it again and again. Test yourself, make up questions, draw mindmaps, recite, or write lists. Use mnemonics.

Final syllables -el -al -le

1. Always use **-le** if the consonant before the **l** has a stick or a tail.

   dabble   tinkle   pimple   rattle   mingle   handle   dangle   bristles
   stable   temple   bible   single   ankle   mangle   shuttle

2. If the letter before **l** has no stick or tail, use **-el**.

   funnel   trowel   quarrel   barrel   squirrel   flannel   easel   gravel   navel   drivel

   Exceptions: **parallel** and words where **zz** is involved.

   dazzle   embezzle   fizzle   nozzle   puzzle

   Use **el** also to keep **c** and **g** soft.

   angel   cancel   Nigel   Angela   Marcel   parcel

3. When the **l** syllable means "to do with" the base word, use **-al**.

   seasonal   tropical   nautical   topical   tyrannical   magical   musical

   -al is also used most commonly when the word is an adjective.

   local   rural   legal   total   central   fatal   royal   equal   menial   trial

   Add the ending **-le**, **-el**, or **-al** to each word below. In the brackets, write the number of the rule which applies (either 1, 2, or 3) from sections 1-3 above.

   wrink ___ [ ]   dimp ___ [ ]   fiction ___ [ ]   tri ___ [ ]
   triang ___ [ ]   chanc ___ [ ]   tunn___ [ ]   addition ___ [ ]
   nov ___ [ ]   grav ___ [ ]

   Make sure you know what these words mean.

4. Complete the sentences below using the correct endings. If in doubt, use a dictionary.

   1. The chann___ tunn___ train is sometimes referred to by the French as "le shutt____ ."

   2. It is terrib___ to consider the rate at which the tropic___ rainforest is being eroded.

   3. Slaves used to be shack___d by a ball and chain round one ank___ .

   4. If you canc___ a medic___ appointment, you may have to wait some time for a new date.

   Your teacher will give you the above sentences for dictation. Write them in your exercise book.

More about -le endings and homophones

1. Homophones are words which sound the same but are spelled differently, and have different meanings.

   Match each homophone with its meaning:

able	a boy's name – brother of Cain
pedal	to interfere
right	to sell or tout
meddle	work with legs
naval	to do with seagoing vessels
peddle	a badge of honor
medal	put pen to paper
write	belly button
navel	opposite of left
Abel	has ability

2. Now read and complete each sentence using the correct homophone:

   1. He looked extremely handsome in his nav_____ uniform, especially when wearing all his war med_____s.

   2. He would start to _____ his autobiography as soon as he was ab_____ after he was discharged from the navy.

   3. The father looked in awe and amazement as the midwife cut the umbilical cord which had attached his newborn child to the placenta. This would later be the baby's nav_____.

   4. He had to ped_____ like fury to catch up with his friends in the twenty-five mile time trial. He had lost touch with them when they turned _____ unexpectedly while he stopped to check his tire which was developing a bulge.

What would you do if you swallowed a light bulb?   Use a candle.

1. Say **earth** **er**, **bear** **A r**, and **ear** **E r**.

What on **ear**th's happened to the b**ear**'s **ear**?

2. Read the following with your teacher and then underline or highlight all of the **e r** words in the passage.

E r rear dear near spear gears fearfully hearing

e r earn pearl early search dearth yearned learned Earl heard

Badgers return to the Earl of Pearl's estate

There had been a dearth of badgers in Earnshaw, so when we heard that they had returned, we set out early in the evening to search for them in earnest.

We hoped to learn that they were still occupying the old earth (or sett) to the north of Pearl Paddock, where we had last seen them. We had to keep very quiet or the badgers would stay in their earth all night and not venture out. We yearned to catch just one glimpse of them and learn more about their nocturnal habits.

More about vowel pattern EAR ear

1. Read the following words with your teacher and then underline or highlight all of the **ear** **E** **r** words in the passage.

ear   hear   shear   year   tear   geared

dreary   cleared   bleary   beard   feared   reared

seared   neared   clearing   earring   appeared   disappeared

Just as we were beginning to fear they would not appear, we heard a rustling sound in the undergrowth and hardly daring to breathe, we suddenly saw an ear and then a black and white snout appear at the entrance to the earth.

Our bleary eyes were becoming used to staring into the gloom when we heard another sound coming from a clearing on our left.

2. What happened next? Can you write a conclusion to the story? Don't forget to plan it first, using a mindmap.

_____

_____

_____

_____

_____

_____

_____

_____

_____

_____

More about vowel pattern ear

1. Read **A r**   bear   wear   tear   swear   pear (fruit)

"I'll swear that bear will use his claws or his jaws to tear the blueberry pies from the string bag hanging on the pear tree. They are thieves. I will wear my bear scaring mask, take my spear, and go out to see if I can frighten him away. If I can't scare him away, I'll tear my hair!"

"Why don't you try banging the two stew pan lids together," suggested Claire.

"I must get a picture of this," she said, crawling out of the tent awkwardly with her photography gear around her neck.

2. Underline all the **A r** words in the above passage.
   Where do you think they were camping?

3. Listen to the teacher. (See page 19.) Write the words in the correct columns.

e r	**A r**	**E r**
_____	_____	_____
_____	_____	_____
_____	_____	_____
_____	_____	_____
_____	_____	_____
_____	_____	_____
_____	_____	_____

More about vowel pattern ear

1. Now read Ogden Nash's poem <u>The Adventures of Isabel</u>

   Isabel met an enormous bear,

   Isabel, Isabel, didn't care,

   The bear was hungry, the bear was ravenous,

   The bear's big mouth was cruel and cavernous.

   The bear said "Isabel, glad to meet you,

   How do, Isabel, now I'll eat you!"

   Isabel, Isabel, didn't worry,

   Isabel didn't scream or scurry

   She washed her hands and she straightened her hair up

   Then Isabel quietly ate the bear up.

2. This poem is written in rhyming couplets. List these rhyming patterns below:

   1. _____ bear _____   _____ care _____

   2. _____   _____

   3. _____   _____

   4. _____   _____

   5. _____   _____

I wonder where fleas go in winter?   Search me.

Reading: -ti -ci -ssi -xi say **sh**

1. In words of more than one syllable **-ti**, **-ci**, **ssi**, and **xi** say **sh** when
   followed by a vowel.
   Underline **ti**, **ci**, **ssi**, and **xi** in the following words. Split into syllables and read.

pro|vin|cial   pa|tience   superficial   crucial   ferocious

commercial   ancient   malicious   auspicious   procession

position   suspicious   facial   efficient   cautious

torrential   officious   passion   superstitious   special

noxious   sufficient   permission   influential   patient

2. Trace and add ous   Trace and add al

   pretenti_____   spati_____   palati_____   marti_____

   delici_____   graci_____   spaci_____   initi_____

   infecti_____   vici_____   offici_____   soci_____

   preci_____   anxi_____   raci_____   essenti_____

Now read the words you have written.

3. Read.

   The bumptious politician was famous for his voracious appetite. He was especially partial to the delicious meals which an ambitious chef sometimes provided for him, unofficially. He had a passion for a certain deliciously nutritious
   confection and was known to eat more than an elegant sufficiency at times.
   He would show his appreciation by graciously and confidentially making a
   substantial financial settlement to this provincial residential hotel.

4. Ask your teacher for a spelling test. (See page 19.) Use your exercise book.

Word search using grid references and definitions

I.

	A	B	C	D	E	F	G	H	I	J	K	L	M	N	O	P	Q	R	S
1	v	o	s	t	r	i	a	m	j	h	u	q	u	a	t	i	n	t	e
2	s	t	o	r	m	u	s	i	c	i	a	n	f	l	i	n	t	e	d
3	m	o	r	p	u	q	u	a	r	t	e	r	l	y	r	e	p	a	y
4	a	t	r	e	a	c	l	e	i	f	t	h	i	n	k	s	g	h	f
5	g	e	l	e	c	t	r	i	c	i	a	n	s	q	u	i	d	p	r
6	i	n	s	e	c	t	o	r	c	h	l	i	g	h	t	i	n	t	o
7	c	o	l	l	e	g	e	t	e	c	h	n	i	c	i	a	n	u	p
8	i	t	y	u	p	p	i	e	n	t	r	a	n	c	e	s	a	i	d
9	a	f	o	u	l	g	j	k	l	s	d	o	i	l	e	y	a	n	t
10	h	n	a	t	h	e	s	t	a	t	i	s	t	i	c	i	a	n	f
11	d	i	e	t	i	c	i	a	n	t	h	o	l	o	g	y	f	o	r
12	k	l	n	o	t	y	u	v	d	r	e	a	l	l	y	n	e	a	t
13	t	e	l	e	p	h	a	n	t	b	e	a	u	t	i	c	i	a	n
14	a	u	d	i	t	i	o	n	o	u	n	a	d	v	e	r	b	u	t
15	u	p	h	y	s	i	c	i	a	n	w	h	o	k	n	o	w	s	i
16	t	r	e	m	e	n	d	o	u	s	c	a	u	s	t	i	c	s	o
17	v	o	i	c	e	o	b	s	t	e	t	r	i	c	i	a	n	o	w
18	x	y	z	p	o	l	i	t	i	c	i	a	n	l	e	a	d	e	r
19	a	c	c	o	m	m	o	d	a	t	i	o	n	t	o	l	e	t	k
20	e	y	e	s	i	g	h	t	o	p	t	i	c	i	a	n	s	e	e

Find these words:

musician   optician   statistician   electrician   dietician   physician
beautician   technician   obstetrician   politician

2. Write the definitions and the grid references for the beginning of each word.

   1. Someone who plays a musical instrument. __E__, __2__ .

   2. Someone who works with electricity ____, ____ .

   > Use your exercise book.

3. List the other words you can find in your exercise book, e.g., tint, storm, music. Copy accurately. There are at least 50 words. Have a competition with a friend to see who can find the most words.

Science vocabulary

Read.

acid	evaporation	organism	diffusion
alkali	gravity	electrolysis	decomposition
neutralize	distillation	reduction	element
chlorophyll	catalyst	displacement	oxidation
molecule	base	photosynthesis	genes

Clues to the crossword puzzle are found on the next page.

Clues for science vocabulary

Across

1. Separation of a compound into elements

3. Units of heredity; made of DNA and part of a chromosome

5. Liberates hydrogen ions in water, turns litmus red, is sour

7. Opposite of oxidation; oxygen is lost from and hydrogen is gained by a substance

11. Neutralizes an alkali

12. Living individual

13. Smallest unit of a chemical compound that can take part in a chemical reaction

14. A compound which neutralizes an acid

15. Plants use of light energy to make food

17. Force that attracts a body to the center of the earth

18. Separation of elements in a compound by electricity

19. Random motion of molecules

20. Reaction whereby a more active metal replaces a less active metal in a compound

Down

2. Combine an acid and base

4. Process which changes a liquid to a gas

6. Green part of plants, absorbs light to provide energy for photosynthesis

8. Addition/reaction of oxygen to metals

9. Substance which increases the rate of a reaction without itself being changed

10. Process of vaporizing a liquid by heating, then condensing and collecting the result

16. Cannot be resolved into a simpler substance by chemical means

A New Dinosaur?

1

A new carnivorous dinosaur from the early Jurassic period has been unearthed on a scree slope 12,000 feet (4000 meters) up in mountains 400 miles (644 kilometers) from the South Pole.

The creature, 24 feet (8 meters) long from nose to tail, is not merely a new species, but a new genus – both dog and wolf are species, but each is a member of the *Canis* genus.

2

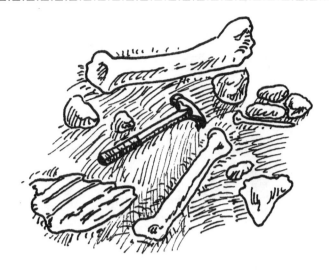

The new dinosaur has been locked in siltstone on the slopes of Mount Kirkpatrick in the Transantarctic mountain range for almost 200 million years. The find confirms the emerging picture of dinosaurs as creatures which could regulate their temperatures – unlike reptiles – and dominate enormous ranges of the planet for more than 150 million years before disappearing 65 million years ago.

3

This specimen had a large head with short horns above its eyes and a large distinctive crest made of thin bone. Its shape has been put together over three years from 100 bits of skull, backbone, pelvis, tail, and one leg. The animal's femur, which measured about a yard (meter) was found on the cliff face. The new dinosaur was called Cryolophosaurus ellioti.

4

The bones had to be chiseled out of tons of rock recovered from the site where geologists with helicopter crews worked at temperatures as low as -58°F (-50°C). Three other species of dinosaur were also discovered at the same site. Nearby scientists have also found fossil tree trunks indicating a world of primitive trees called gymnosperms.

5

After the early Jurassic period a global change took place. When Cryolophosaurus died, the site would have been a low-lying flood plain or estuary, and the continent would have been what is now called Gondwana – a vast amalgam of Africa, South America, Australia, India, and present-day Antarctica.

6

The discovery was no surprise to the experts. Some dinosaurs were found on the north slope of Alaska in 1987, so it was no surprise to discover them poles apart, at either end of the world. We now know that they were very widespread.

7

Answer the following questions:

1. Look in an *atlas* to pinpoint just where this creature was discovered.

2. What are the definitions of a) an herbivore and b) a carnivore?

3. What do you think the *ellioti* part of the dinosaur's name referred to?

4. Find a time line and see where the Jurassic period comes in relation to present day.

5. What is the study of fossils called?

6. Which bone is the *femur*?

7. Find out what the syllables *cryo, loph,* and *saurus* mean.

8. Imagine you have discovered a new creature. Describe it and name it.

8

Suffix -or

Oh, horr**or**! Call the doct**or**!

1. Auditory Introduction. (See page 13.)
2. Visual Introduction. (See page 13.)
3. Say **doctor** . The sound is the same as pepper .
4. Introduce the clueword and Spelling/Reading Cards.

5. Highlight the **or** and practice reading these words. When you are ready, read the words to your teacher.

actor	tractor	sponsor	anchor
cursor	factor	juror	motor
tutor	advisor	author	ambassador
supervisor	calculator	indicator	bachelor

6. Listen as your teacher gives you some words. (See page 19.) Write **or** in the box if you hear ə r in the word.

1	2	3	4	5	6	7	8	9	10

More about suffix -or

1. Highlight **or** and read.

actor	anchor	donor	tutor	supervisor	bachelor
tractor	cursor	juror	advisor	calculator	ambassador
sponsor	factor	motor	author	indicator	

2. Trace and then copy each word twice. Copy the sentence twice in your exercise book. Check the one you prefer.

or _____ _____   doctor _____ _____

mirror _____ _____

Seniors should remember that juniors are not always inferior.

3. The suffix **or** is often added to a root verb to mean the person or thing doing the action. Example: to act (verb)... actor (noun)... the person doing the acting. Change these verbs into nouns. Remember the rules for adding suffixes and check your spellings by **v c** patterning and splitting.

advise___advisor___   visit_____   sail_____

calculate_____   imitate_____   ventilate_____

invent_____   translate_____   indicate_____

4. All multisyllable words will have one syllable which is stressed or spoken louder than the others. Example: **pep**per **doc**tor **ham**mer **trac**tor **ed**itor **op**erator **swim**mer in**ven**tor **tea**cher be**gin**ner sur**vi**vor

In one syllable words, the whole word is stressed.

Example: **curb   corn   first**

Listen to the teacher and underline the stressed syllable in each word. (see page 19.)

thirty   turnip   injection

calculator   senator   adventurer   malnutrition

More about or in unstressed syllables

1. Read and notice the different sounds.

or in *stressed* syllables says **o r**

born **corps** **torn** **mor**ning
force **shor**tage **glor**y **scorn**

or in unstressed syllables says **ə r**

sponsor **mon**itor ab**duc**tor
ivory **mem**ory **gov**ernor **tail**or

er in *stressed* syllables says **e r**

term **verse** **fern** dis**perse**
fertile **ver**satile **er**gonomics

er in unstressed syllables says **ə r**

sub**scri**ber con**den**ser **boi**ler
fertilizer **ligh**ter **syn**thesizer

Read or record each word and write it in the correct column.

equator	hornet	ancestor	organ	protractor	scorn
important	collector	absorb	dictator	director	short
torment	morsel	corner	janitor	equator	born

or **o r**

_____

_____

_____

_____

_____

_____

_____

or **ə r**

_____

_____

_____

_____

_____

_____

_____

_____

_____

More about or in unstressed syllables

1. Read. Punctuate and add capital letters.

A Famous Doctor. david livingstone grew up in scotland from the age of 10 he worked in cotton mills at 23 he managed to attend andersons college after this he studied medicine at glasgow university and graduated as a doctor later he applied to the london missionary society which sent him to south africa he traveled 400 miles among the native tribes healing them and preaching the christian gospels during his explorations he discovered the mighty zambesi river and in 1855 the victoria falls which he named after queen victoria of great britain he made other amazing journeys the last of which was an attempt to discover the source of the nile when he died in 1873 his heart was buried in africa but his body was carried to zanzibar and then shipped to england and buried in westminster abbey

You should have found 9 periods and 35 capital letters missing.
Did you find the (') and the (,)s ?

2. Working from left to right, identify the letters above the first 1, 2, 3, 4, and 5.
What word have you spelled? __ __ __ __ __

S	H	N	D	U	A	C	L	V	K	M	I	X	W	E
1	1	2	1	2	3	1	2	3	4	1	2	3	4	5

3. Use the same formula to identify the name of a large boa constrictor.

__ __ __ __ __ __ __ __

A	B	N	U	V	A	E	R	M	C	K	I	D	L	O	T	H	E
1	1	2	1	2	3	1	2	3	4	1	2	3	4	5	1	2	3
J	A	N	U	M	B	E	R	S	D	A	N	D	Z	F	O	R	A
4	5	6	1	2	3	4	5	6	7	1	2	3	4	5	6	7	8

4. Find out more about constrictors. How do they kill their prey?

R S

Have you heard the joke about the magic tractor?

It drove down the road and turned into a field.

More about -or

A w**or**m w**or**king on the w**or**ld's w**or**st w**or**ds.

1. Auditory Introduction. (See page 13.)
2. Visual Introduction. (See page 13.)
3. When **or** comes after the letter **w** it is usually pronounced ▰ə r▶.
4. Introduce the clueword and Spelling/Reading Cards.

5. Highlight the **or** and practice reading these words. When you are ready, read the words to your teacher.

worm	work	word	wording	wordy
worker	world	wormy	worry	worship
worst	worth	worthy	worse	worsen

6. Practice this sentence and be ready for dictation.

A worm working on the world's worst words.

World's worst words

1. These spelling patterns are not making their usual sounds because they are in unstressed syllables. Read.

space **sp A s** but *palace* **p a l i s**

menace   **sol**ace   **furn**ace   **grim**ace   **pref**ace

surface   **ter**race   **neck**lace   **pop**ulace

late **l A t** but *certificate* **s ə r t i f i k i t**

chocolate   ap**pro**priate   ap**pro**ximate   **ad**equate   bi**car**bonate

doctorate   con**sid**erate   **al**ternate   **ag**gregate   **cor**porate

desperate

rain **r A n** but *mountain* **m ou n t i n**

fountain   **cur**tain   **cer**tain   **cap**tain   **vill**ain

bargain   **Brit**ain   ODD WORD main**tain**

mice **m I s** but *notice* **n O t i s**

office   **crev**ice   **jus**tice   **prac**tice   ac**com**plice

hospice   **cap**tive   **cur**sive   e**va**sive   **fes**tive

passive   **ad**ditive   **en**gine   i**mag**ine   ex**am**ine

genuine   **her**oine   **jas**mine

ALSO   **min**ute   **lett**uce   **tor**toise

2. **PUZZLES**

In place of the 7 X's, put something cold to drink, that begins with an "L." If correct you will have made 7 new words. Read the new words downward.

```
P D I H A M O F
L X X X X X X X
Y N P B T R D W
```

FIGURE IT OUT

Use the code to unlock the sentence. Change numbers to letters.

5 23941 HAS 98 7215 HOW 68 28 DIFFICULT SUMS.
     (?5?)   (?8?)   (27??74???)

Word play

1. Form a new word from another by changing the first letter.

die . . . tie   cone . . . bone

hay . . . . _____   train . . . . _____

beach. . . _____   coy. . . . . _____

niece . . . _____   glue . . . . _____

tumble . . _____   house . . . _____

gaunt . . . _____   boast . . . _____

hoist. . . . _____   sail. . . . . _____

pew . . . . _____   tight . . . . _____

found . . . _____   turning . . _____

look . . . . _____   patch . . . _____

south . . . _____   raw . . . . _____

tow . . . . _____

2. Read the following words. Underline the synonym in brackets which is similar in meaning to the word on the left.

absurd   [foolish, empty, surprising]   fear   [phobia, hat, irritation]

cyclone   [typhoon, storm, moped]   globe [ball, light, sphere]

decipher [understand, read, decode]   real   [authentic, alive, dance]

chief   [opinion, Indian, principal]   voice [believe, utter, amuse]

3. Choose 4 words form Section 2 and write a sentence using each word.

_____

_____

_____

_____

_____

_____

_____

_____

_____

Word play, cont.

1. Trace and fill in the letters **or, au,** or **aw.**

br____n	th____n	p____ses	c____ght
l____nch	spr____led	st____med	scr____ny
b____n	c____ds	t____ght	t____nt
l____ful	dr____n	cr____ling	c____ses
f____ds	p____nch	j____nt	f____med
dr____led	____ful	t____ny	tr____ling

Now link the rhyming pairs in each group. Underline all the suffixes you can find. There are 14.

2. Join the syllables and read these words.

ar	is	tra
or	u	sion
trans	ches	ate
sit	plo	tect
di	ver	try
ex	chi	sion
chem	fu	sion

Writing poetry

1. Haiku poetry (pronounced **h I k oo**) is a form of poetry which the Japanese have been writing for hundreds of years. It is like a snapshot made with your camera, but the picture is in words. Traditionally, it follows a three line verse with a five, seven, five syllable format like this:

On a lonely branch (5)	Still, softly staring
An owl hoots so eerily (7)	Lion suddenly starting
Saying "Beware mouse" (5)	Gives chase for supper

You do not need to stick strictly to the 5, 7, 5 syllable pattern at first, but as you get better at writing poetry with practice, you could try this formula.

You should however:

- Stick to the three line verse.
- Start a new line when you pause.
- Make the last line shorter than the other two.
- Don't use any more words than necessary.
- Every word must be vital to the whole.
- Look at more examples by other poets.

> *First Haiku of Spring*
> cuck oo cuck oo cuck
> oo cuck oo cuck oo cuck oo
> cuck oo cuck oo cuck
>
> by Roger McGough

You may leave out the boring words such as **like**, **the**, **this**, **is**, **then**, and **there**.

2. Do you know about:
   - alliteration? This is when words in the lines start with the same sound.
     Example: **S**till, **s**oftly **s**taring
   - onomatopoeia? This is when the sound echoes the sense of the poem.
     Example: **crackle**, **sizzle**, **hiss**, **howl**, **hoot**, **toot**, **clink**

   These are devices you can use to make your poems much more interesting.

3. Write your own Haiku. This is good practice.

_____ _____ _____ _____ _____

_____ _____ _____ _____ _____ _____

_____ _____ _____ _____ _____

Writing poetry, cont.

1. Write a poem. Think of something visual, beautiful, or moving. Think of something that makes you feel angry, puzzled, worried, or sad.

   Now change papers with your friend. Read each other's poems and see what you think about them. Can you think of any way they could be improved? Show your friend the ideas you consider to be an improvement. Your friend must not be made to change his/her poem unless he/she agrees that your ideas are an improvement.

   _____ _____ _____ _____

   _____ _____ _____ _____ _____

   _____ _____ _____ _____

2. Listen to the teacher read an example of onomatopoeia in a poem. (See page 19.) It is called the "From a Railway Carriage" by Robert Louis Stevenson. Talk to your teacher or your friends about the poem.

   The Traditional Grammarian as Poet
   Haiku, you ku, he
   She, or it kus, we ku, you
   Ku, they Ku. Thang ku.
   by Ted Hipple

Sound Pictures ——→ Words

Make the Sound Pictures, write the words.

1. Use Spelling Pack cards to make these Sound Pictures.	2. Turn the cards over. Tell your hand what to write, naming the letters.	3. Write the word.
Look Say	Listen Name the letters	Write
i n v A zh'n	– i-n-v-a-s-i-o-n –	invasion
1. e k s pl O zh'n		1.
2. E m u l sh'n		2.
3. r e s k U		3.
4. kl oo		4.
5. n E		5.
6. er th		6.
7. k e m i s tr E		7.
8. sh a m p A n		8.
9. m o s k		9.
10. n e t'l		10.
11. sp A sh u s		11.
12. n U t r i sh u s		12.

Vowel pattern ou with different sounds

The **you**ng c**ou**ple loved s**ou**p with cr**ou**tons.

1. Auditory Introduction. (See page 13.)
2. Visual Introduction. (See page 13.)
3. Say **couple** **U** **soup** **OO**.
4. Introduce the clueword and Reading/Spelling Cards.

5. Highlight **ou** and practice reading these words. When you are ready, read the words to your teacher.

soup	toucan	croup	croutons	uncouth
group	youth	goulash	troupe	wound

What sound did **ou** make in the above words?_____

6. Highlight **ou** and practice reading these words. When you are ready, read the words to your teacher.

couple	country	double	cousins	southern
courage	trouble	young	touch	youngster

What sound did **ou** make in the above words?_____

More about vowel pattern ou with different sounds

1. In these three words, **ou** has a different sound.

ou   🔲

should   could   would

2. Underline the **ou** words in the first paragraph writing the 🔲 or 🔲 sound picture above the word. Now insert the correct **ou** words in the remainder of the passage. (Look at page 171 sections 5 and 6.) You may use some words more than once.

The elderly northern cousins from the country kept inviting their youthful southern cousins with their lively youngsters to visit them. The southern cousins kept making excuses because of their passion for goulash soup. It was something which never appeared on the menu at the northern dinner table.

Eventually the _____ _____ felt they could no longer avoid the pressing invitation. Taking their _____ in both hands, they asked if their northern counterparts would object to their bringing their own _____ with them. The northerners were only too delighted. Before they left for the north, the _____ family cautiously _____-checked that they had made their home safe from a _____ of _____ and malicious _____s who were reported to be prowling the neighborhood.

On arrival at the palatial estate the northerners were presented with a huge tureen of _____ and a separate bowl of _____ , the beneficial properties of which were highly rec-ommended. The _____ was appreciated and the whole _____ of the Mouton family dined with gusto, had _____ helpings and the recipe was requested by the north-ern relatives who declared that _____ _____ with _____ would be a part of their regular diet in future.

More about vowel pattern ou

1. Draw a picture for each word below:

croutons	coupons	toucan	toupee

2. Listen to your teacher. (See page 20.) Write the words in the correct columns below:

ou **U**   ou **OO**

_____   _____

_____   _____

_____   _____

_____   _____

_____   _____

3. Note these odd words:

canoe **k** **a** **n** **OO**   shoe **s h** **OO**   lasso **l** **a** **s** **OO**

4. See if you can make up a poem, story, or joke using the **ou** letter pattern saying **U** or **OO**.

How many **ou** **U** or **OO** sounds can you include?

Congratulate yourself if you can manage ten.

5. This is the 3rd choice for spelling **OO** sounds in the main part of words.

This soup is terrible.
Call the manager.

Waiter:
He won't eat it either, sir.

OO
ou
soup

Long vowel pattern eigh and ei

The **rei**ndeer pulls the w**eigh**t of the sl**eigh**.

1. Auditory Introduction. (See page 13.)
2. Visual Introduction. (See page 13.)
3. Say **weight** **A**. Say **reindeer** **A**. The **eigh** and **ei** both have the same sound as alphabetical name A.
4. Introduce the clueword and Reading/Spelling Cards.

5. Highlight **eigh** and practice reading these words. When you are ready, read the words to your teacher.

weight	neighbor	neighborhood
eight	eighty	freight
eighteen	sleigh	weigh

6. Highlight **ei** and practice reading these words. When you are ready, read the words to your teacher.

vein	rein	veil	deign	feign
skein	seine	reigns	surveillant	geisha

More about long vowel pattern eigh and ei

1. Trace and fill in **ei** A.

n_____ghbors   g_____sha   f_____gn

w_____ght   b_____ge   n_____ghs

fr_____ght   surv_____llance

Read the words you have made. Look up any words you do not know in your dictionary.

2. Listen to the teacher. (See page 20.) Write a number 1 in the box of the first word you hear, a 2 in the box of the second word and so on.

typhoon ☐	ate ☐	slay ☐
deign ☐	reins ☐	eighty ☐
vale ☐	weight ☐	wait ☐
reigns ☐	vain ☐	their ☐
way ☐	weigh ☐	veil ☐
sleigh ☐	vein ☐	there ☐
vane ☐	rains ☐	Dane ☐

3. The teacher will read 10 words from Section 2.
Write them in your exercise book.

More about long vowel pattern ei

1. Complete the following sentences. (Use the words from page 175.)

   1. The _____ of Queen Victoria lasted for 64 years.

   2. After _____ years living next door to us, our _____ are moving.

   3. At _____ pounds, that dog is seriously over_____ .

   4. The horse _____ as the rider _____ him in.

   5. The _____ train carries a cargo of coal.

   6. _____s carry blood back to the heart.

   7. Please _____, I'm not ready to go.

   8. Look over there, I see _____ reindeer.

   9. My next door _____ are good friends.

2. You have now learned a 3rd way to spell **A** in the main part of words.

Long Vowel Sound Picture	Open syllable	Main part of word				End of the word One syllable word	
		1st try	2nd try	3rd try	4th try	4th try	1st try
A	**A** v c v a acorn	**A** a – e cake	**A** ai tail	**A** eigh weight	**A** ei reindeer	**A** ay tray	**A**

A ei weight

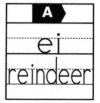
A ei reindeer

Long vowel pattern ei

Keith paints the c**ei**ling.

1. Auditory Introduction. (See page 13.)
2. Visual Introduction. (See page 13.)
3. Say **ceiling** **E** . **ei** can also say the long vowel sound **E** .
4. Introduce the clueword and Reading/Spelling Cards.

5. Highlight the **ei** and practice reading these words. Note the **ei** after **c** says **E** . Read these words to your teacher.

receipt	deceive	conceit	perceive
receive	receiver	conceive	deceit

*Remember the spelling rhyme: **i** before **e** except after **c**.*

6. Words that break the rule:

caffeine	protein	either	seize
seizure	inveigle	Neil	Sheila
leisure	neither	weird	sheik

More about long vowel pattern ei

Read.

In the hurly-burly turmoil of the rush hour at Kings Cross Station, Paul Floyd searched anxiously for his elderly aunt, a pensioner, who was arriving for her autumn visit on the eighteen thirty-two from Thurso in the north.

At last he spotted his loyal relation struggling under the weight of a ridiculously heavy case. He dropped his new briefcase and surged forward with the crowd to greet her.

1

He kissed her awkwardly and as they walked up the platform arm in arm, happy to be in each other's company again, Paul remembered his briefcase.

It won't surprise you to learn that the briefcase had vanished and with it many important papers connected with his work as a lawyer at Lloyd, Phillips, and Andrews. Paul left his aunt and went to find or phone a police officer. He soon found one. In fact, he found several. There was great excitement and commotion outside the station as police were keeping people away from an army mechanic who was in the middle of the road fiddling with a technical device which he was attaching to a new briefcase.

2

"I want to report a missing briefcase," Paul mumbled nervously to a police officer with a moustache who looked like the chief. "I think a thief purloined it!"

His words were drowned out by a loud explosion. Tiny pieces of blue leather blew sky-high and charred papers began to drift down to earth.

"And can you give me a description of this briefcase?"

"It's blue leather," muttered Paul.

3

A sign above his head read: Unattended luggage will be confiscated.

What do you think happened next? Use a mindmap to note your ideas and then write your own continuation of the story in your exercise book. Remember to use paragraphs. Proofread your work, correcting spelling and punctuation. Check for word order or words left out.

4

ie and ei choices

1. Listen to the teacher. (See page 20.) Copy the headings for **E▷** in the main part of words into your exercise book. Write the words you hear in the correct columns.

Long Vowel Sound Picture	Main part of word				
	1st try **E▷**	2nd try **E▷**	3rd try **E▷**	4th try **E▷**	5th try **E▷**
E▷	ee	ea	e – e	ie	ei

ODD WORDS: foreign   sovereign

2. Listen to the teacher and fill in the missing **ie** or **ei** words below. If you prefer you may write the sentences in your exercise book.

   1. It is difficult to _____ that he has lost so much _____.

   2. The _____ woman ignored his remarks about her _____ accent.

   3. The _____ of police introduced electronic _____ techniques in order to _____ the _____.

   4. He _____ a small fortune for the master _____ which was auctioned to a wealthy _____.

   5. Despite _____ competition, he _____ first place.

   6. His _____ picked up the _____ when the phone rang.

3. Checking a receipt. Discuss these questions with your teacher.

   What is a *receipt*?

   What does *retain* mean?

   What is a *guarantee*?

   Why should you keep a receipt?

THE VILLAGE SHOE SHOP
6/11/00
CUSTOMER RECEIPT COPY
5764 LADIES SHOES $39.95
TOTAL AMOUNT TENDERED $40.00
CHANGE GIVEN $ .05
RETAIN YOUR RECEIPT
THIS IS YOUR GUARANTEE

Why do bank managers carry briefcases?   Because briefcases won't walk.

Vowel digraph ey and irregular sound ey

1. Say **donkey** E grey A .

   This is the second choice for A sounds at the end of words.

   Little gr**ey** donk**ey**.

2. Ask for help if you find it difficult to read these words.

   E

monkey	pulley	trolley
barley	parsley	kidney
honey	turkey	chimney
whiskey	jockey	journey

   A

they	prey	obey
grey	survey	whey
disobey	convey	purvey

3. Trace filling in E and read.   A

   voll____   blarn____   surv____   disob____

   jers____   vall____   wh____   ospr____

   gall____   medl____   conv____   th____

Vowel digraph ey and irregular sound ey, cont.

1. Write the solutions to the following clues. They are all **ey** or ⬢A⬢ words.

   1. An animal that swings through the trees. _____

   2. Mrs. Johnson raises _____ bees.

   3. Little Miss Muffet ate them with curds. _____

   4. Game played with sticks. _____

   5. When you break the rules you _____ .

   6. A cereal for making soup or feeding cattle. _____

   7. Eaten, especially at Christmas or Thanksgiving. _____

2. Use each of the following words in a sentence.

   chimney   jockey   they   obey

   1. _____
   _____

   2. _____
   _____

   3. _____
   _____

   4. _____
   _____

3. **ea** saying ⬢A⬢.
   A **break** for lunch
   with **steak** and
   chips is **great**.

What are assets?

Little donkeys.

ey
grey

Using prefixes and suffixes to change meaning

1. Divide each word into a root word, prefix, and suffix.

	Prefix	Root word	Suffix
replacement	_____	_____	_____
disgraceful	_____	_____	_____
unluckily	_____	_____	_____
beloved	_____	_____	_____
adventurer	_____	_____	_____
explainable	_____	_____	_____
preconditions	_____	_____	_____
indistinctness	_____	_____	_____
confirming	_____	_____	_____

2. Use these prefixes to change the meanings of these words.

com   dis   ex   il   im   in   ir   re   un

____sane	____certain	____popular	____current
____human	____aware	____probable	____spire
____perfect	____regular	____gratitude	____pose
____efficient	____usual	____regard	____important
____obedient	____change	____continue	____claim
____favorable	____approve	____considerate	____proper
____press	____equality	____similar	____orderly
____frequent	____legal	____patient	____necessary

3. Turn these nouns into adjectives by adding a suffix.

–ic   –ful   –esque   –al   –ive   –ous   –able

	adjective	noun	adjective to be changed
a	_____	sound	metal
a	_____	craftsman	skill
a	_____	garden	picture
an	_____	remedy	effect
an	_____	man	athlete
an	_____	car	expense
a	_____	release	mercy
an	_____	death	accident
a	_____	plant	poison
a	_____	dog	faith

Suffix -ar

A dog coll**ar**? How peculi**ar**!

1. Auditory Introduction. (See page 13.)
2. Visual Introduction. (See page 13.)
3. Say **collar** ⟨ə r⟩. The sound is the same as **pepper** ⟨ə r⟩.
   When **-ar** is in an unstressed syllable it is pronounced ⟨ə r⟩.
4. Introduce the clueword and Spelling/Reading Cards.

5. Highlight the **-ar** and practice reading these words. When you are ready,
   read the words to your teacher.

beggar	lunar	popular	grammar
dollar	collar	nectar	cellar
cedar	pillar	polar	solar

6. Listen as your teacher gives you some words. (See page 20.) Write **-ar** in the
   box if you hear ⟨ə r⟩ in the word.

1	2	3	4	5	6	7	8

More about suffix -ar

1. Trace filling in ar and read.

doll____   burgl____   rectangul____   schol____

alt____   vulg____   pill____   popul____

muscul____   simil____   cell____   calend____

2. Listen to the teacher. (See page 20.) Number the words as you hear them.

aggressor ☐   beggar ☐   professor ☐

perpendicular ☐   subscriber ☐   alligator ☐

blackmailer ☐   bullfighter ☐   adviser ☐

dictator ☐   chronometer ☐   molecular ☐

activator ☐   grammar ☐   mortar ☐

Underline the letters making the [ə r] sound. They are: ____ , ____ , ____ .

3. Trace and then copy the sentence twice. Check the best one.

The vicar fastened his circular collar and knelt at the altar.

_____

_____

_____

4. Read or record the words and notice the difference that _STRESS_ makes to the sounds.

STRESSED

er saying [e r]	or saying [o r]	ar saying [a r]
<u>her</u>bicide	<u>mor</u>sel	<u>char</u>ming
p<u>er</u>manent	<u>cor</u>tex	emb<u>ar</u>king

NOT STRESSED

er saying [ə r]	or saying [ə r]	ar saying [ə r]
fea<u>ther</u>	inspec<u>tor</u>	<u>vineg</u>ar
<u>tre</u>asur<u>er</u>	imp<u>ost</u>or	parti<u>cu</u>l<u>ar</u>

Terror in the Cellar

1

Doctor Tendercare and Professor Innovator were at their regular monthly meeting. They were discussing the possibility of modifying the production of their new remedy for stomach ulcers. They always enjoyed talking over a quiet dinner and usually met in the impressive dining room of the professor's large mansion. Mrs. Calendar, the professor's housekeeper, served the meal in her usual quietly efficient manner. She was a "cordon bleu" chef and could be relied upon to produce wonderful meals. That night they were treated to avocado pear and prawn cocktail as a starter, followed by mandarin orange sorbet. The main course was lobster thermidor with a fresh green salad covered in virgin olive oil and balsamic vinegar.

2

Just at the moment when they were starting the dessert, which was sherry trifle, there was a sudden crashing sound, followed by a loud explosion. They both jumped with fright and the doctor, who had been about to put a spoonful of custard into his mouth, jerked his spoon violently, and flicked the custard unceremoniously onto the professor's collar.

3

Ignoring this faux pas both men made their way cautiously down the narrow steps to the cellar which doubled as the professor's laboratory. There they discovered an uninvited visitor. The terrified burglar had stumbled into the professor's workbench, upsetting the apparatus for his latest experiment. His escape through the coal chute was now blocked by brightly burning chemicals which had been scattered by the explosion.

4

"Blundering, cowardly, thief!" shouted the professor angrily, as he overpowered the intruder. "I ought to subject you to some agonizing tests." The doctor hurried to fetch the fire extinguisher.

"Calm down!" he cautioned, "You're frightening the mice."
Before he could lay his hands on the canister a most peculiar thing happened...

5

1. Complete the story making it as vivid and imaginative as you can by using lots of adjectives.

2. Why did the professor keep mice?

3. Do you think animals should be used in experiments?
   Debate this with a friend or in a group.
   How else might medicine progress?

6

Vowel digraphs eu ui oe

Don't drink and drive in **Eu**rope, stick to fr**ui**t j**ui**ce, **J**o**e**!

1. Auditory Introduction. (See page 13.)
2. Visual Introduction. (See page 13.)
3. Say **Europe** **U**▶. The sound is the same as stew.

   Say **fruit** **OO**▶. The sound is the same as spoon.

   Say **toe** **O**▶. The sound is the same as goat.
4. Introduce the clueword and Reading/Spelling Cards.

5. Highlight the **eu** in each word. Read the words to your teacher.

feud	neutral	neuron	eulogy	euthanasia
neurologist	neurology	pneumonia	eureka	deuce
eucalyptus	neuter	maneuver	teutonic	euphemism
Eucharist	heuristic	Euclid	therapeutic	Europe
Eunice	Eustace	Euthenics	eurythmy	pharmaceutical

More about vowel digraphs eu ui oe

1. Highlight the **ui** in each word. Read the words to your teacher.

    fruit   suit   bruise   cruise   juice

    sluice   suitable   suitcase   unsuitable   unsuitably

2. Highlight the **oe** in each word. Read the words to your teacher.

    Joe   hoe   woe   toe   doe

    roe   floe   sloe   aloe   foe

    throes   tiptoe   mistletoe   oboe

3. Listen as your teacher reads this story. (See page 20.) Fill in the blanks to complete the story, using the words above to help you.

_____ and _____ met on a _____ aboard the S. S. Eureka. _____ first noticed _____ during a competition when he made a fool of himself to gain her attention and accidentally stood on her foot. This result-ed in a painful _____ on her big _____. He tried to pour oil on trou-bled water by bringing her a _____ cocktail made of _____ and lime and lemon _____ while apologizing profusely. Unfortunately, the _____ caused inflammation and swelling which masked a serious condi-tion, subsequently diagnosed by a _____. _____ filed a _____ to sue _____ who was sadly unable to appear in court as he was suffering from _____. Eunice was full of _____ when she heard of _____'s serious condition and the _____ was dropped. She visited him daily, doing many helpful tasks like _____ing his garden. She took her _____ and played peaceful music to try to help him to relax and recover.

What do disc jockeys wear?

R S

Tracksuits.

U ▶
eu
Europe

O ▶
oe
toe

Handwriting Practice
Trace and copy.

Sleight of hand is designed to deceive.

The knight calmly drew his sword.

A couple of puppies means double trouble.

I am a beautician Madam, not a magician.

Here's to the inventor of the pocket calculator.

Must popular males be muscular to gain favor?

Travel through the tunnel to the local temple.

Some of the famous and fabulous are ridiculous.

You cannot be anxious, superstitious, and religious.

Champagne caused him a chronic stomachache.

Dynamic pyramid type words

More **i** and **I** sounds spelled y and y-e.

1. You have learned about **y** saying **i** or **I** at the end of words in *Book 4*, when you learned **baby** **i**. **y** can also say the **i** or **I** sound in the middle of words.

   Say **tympany** **i**
   xylophone **I**
   style **I**.

   The **ty**mpanist played the x**y**lophone with st**y**le!

2. Read or record the words on your tape:

y **i**

physics	chlorophyll	gypsy	gymnastics
physicist	Styx	hypnotic	hypnotist
physician	lymphatic	systemic	larynx
lyrics	mysterious	nymph	Egypt
dyslexic	system	mystery	Egyptians
physique	systematic	symposium	physiotherapist
pyramid	lymph	hysteria	photosynthesis

y **I**

hyphen	gyro	cypher	dynamic
typhoon	gyrate	psychiatry	dynamite
typhoid	gyration	cypress	nylon
byzantine	psychology	cyclone	psyche

y - e **I**

tyre	pyre	tyke	hype
style	dyke	megabyte	breathalyze
type	byte	analyze	Sykes
Tyne	soundbyte	enzyme	rhyme

Dynamic pyramid type words, cont.

1. Read.

The physiotherapist, the psychologist, the hypnotist, and the gymnast were all invited to a symposium in Washington D.C. about the mysteries of the relationship between psychology and the physiology of the human body. They wished to analyze the theory that the psychological welfare of human beings and animals has an influence on physical growth and development. Each therapist was interested in delving into the dynamics of their colleagues' different disciplines in order to gain a clearer understanding of the secrets of the human psyche and its effect on the human physique.

2. See if you can write a passage which is amusing and incredible using as many of the words as possible from Section 2 on page 192.

_____

_____

_____

_____

_____

_____

_____

_____

_____

_____

_____

_____

_____

_____

_____

Use another page if necessary.

3. Make up a rhyme or tell someone your favorite joke.

R S

A

y–e
style

Grammar families

To play the following games, you will need copies of pages 195-200 mounted on cardstock and cutout and an egg timer or stopwatch.

GAME ONE- You will need the cards from pages 195-198. Play as Family Fours. The pack is placed facedown in the middle of the table. Each player in turn picks up a card, reads it and places it faceup in front of him/her. When a player recognizes that his/her card belongs to a grammar family which is represented by a card or cards in front of another player, he/she may ask for those cards and claim them as his/her own. The person who picks up the fourth card is entitled to claim the whole family. The winner is the player who collects the most families.

GAME TWO- Draw the following table in your exercise book. You will also need the cards from pages 195-198.

VERB	NOUN	ADJECTIVE	MY NOUN	MY VERB	ADVERB
example					
receive	reception	receptive	audience	listened	receptively
destroy	destruction	destructive	child	hammered	destructively

The pack of cards is placed facedown in the middle of the table. Player 1 picks up a card. The egg timer/stopwatch is set and all players then see if they can think of the other members of that card's grammar family. They may also think of an appropriate noun (My Noun) to go with the adjective and an appropriate verb (My Verb) to go with the adverb. The player whose turn it is earns 2 points for each family member he/she predicts correctly and 3 bonus points if he/she has thought of a good extra noun and verb to go in the "My Noun/Verb" columns. The other players can also earn bonus points of 1 and 2 respectively, if they were correct. Players should keep their answers to themselves as they will be useful later in the game when other family cards in the same family come up. As the game progresses, play will become quicker and easier since the words have already been rehearsed. The winner is the player with the most points.

GAME THREE – SENSIBLE, STIMULATING SENTENCES. You will need the cards from pages 195-200. The pack is sorted into separate stacks of VERBS, NOUNS, ADJECTIVES, and ADVERBS. Each pack is shuffled. The packs of PREPOSITIONS, CONJUNCTIONS, PRONOUNS, and TENSES are added making eight separate stacks of cards.

Each player in turn takes a card off the top of each stack making 8 cards in all. The player then tries to write or say a good sentence using as many of the words as he/she can and in the appropriate tense (2 points per word). Bonus points on a sliding scale are earned according to how many words have been used, e.g., 2 extra points for 4 words used, 3 for 6, and a jackpot of 10 extra points for a full house. The teacher should decide how long each student has to complete the task. Use an egg timer or stopwatch. The other players may attempt the task as well earning 1 bonus point for each word used.

This game can be modified to suit the ability of the students. Simplify the game by using only 2 or 3 categories of words at a time.

actively *adv.*	active *adj.*	an action *n.*	to act *v.*
creatively *adv.*	creative *adj.*	a creation *n.*	to create *v.*
constructively *adv.*	constructive *adj.*	a construction *n.*	to construct *v.*
thoughtfully *adv.*	thoughtful *adj.*	a thought *n.*	to think *v.*
responsively *adv.*	responsive *adj.*	a response *n.*	to respond *v.*
divisively *adv.*	divisive *adj.*	a division *n.*	to divide *v.*

v.	n.	adj.	adv.
to ice	the ice	icy	icily
to compete	a competition	competitive	competitively
to beautify	the beauty	beautiful	beautifully
to explode	an explosion	explosive	explosively
to deceive	the deception	deceptive	deceptively
to imagine	imagination	imaginative	imaginatively

v.	n.	adj.	adv.
to photograph	a photographer	photographic	photographically
to invent	an invention	inventive	inventively
to falsify	falsehood	falsified	falsely
to threaten	a threat	threatening	threateningly
to sense	a sensation	sensational	sensitively
to converse	a conversation	conversational	conversationally

characteristically *adv.*	descriptively *adv.*	resentfully *adv.*	receptively *adv.*	spectacularly *adv.*	destructively *adv.*
characteristic *adj.*	descriptive *adj.*	resentful *adj.*	receptive *adj.*	spectacular *adj.*	destructive *adj.*
a character *n.*	description *n.*	resentment *n.*	the reception *n.*	a spectacle *n.*	the destruction *n.*
to characterize *v.*	to describe *v.*	to resent *v.*	to receive *v.*	to spectate *v.*	to destroy *v.*

present *tense*	past *tense*	future *tense*	present *tense*	past *tense*	future *tense*
he *pron.*	him *pron.*	me *pron.*	it *pron.*	they *pron.*	them *pron.*
and *conj.*	if *conj.*	although *conj.*	but *conj.*	because *conj.*	when *conj.*
with *prep.*	between *prep.*	below *prep.*	in *prep.*	across *prep.*	behind *prep.*

present *tense*	past *tense*	future *tense*	present *tense*	past *tense*	future *tense*
you *pron.*	I *pron.*	who *pron.*	she *pron.*	her *pron.*	everyone *pron.*
unless *conj.*	so *conj.*	or *conj.*	and *conj.*	but *conj.*	because *conj.*
on *prep.*	through *prep.*	from *prep.*	over *prep.*	under *prep.*	near *prep.*

Read this passage from *The Silver Sword* by Ian Serraillier

The book is about four Polish children escaping to
Switzerland during the Second World War.

1

The current was swift. In the darkness the great wooded
hills swept by. For a moment the moon peeped from a cloud
and turned the rippling surface of the stream to silver.

"Stay away, moon," Ruth muttered. "Don't come out again
till we've passed the village."

Side by side, the two canoes sped on. On the left bank the
line of the hills curved downward. Were those dim shapes
houses? Had they reached the village?

2

Again the moon appeared. It had chosen quite the wrong moment, for this was indeed the village, with houses crowded about both banks, and on the left bank suddenly an open space with lorries in it. They were so close together that they were almost touching and there were several rows of them. These must be the lorries that were to take the Polish refugees back to Poland. With a tightening of fear in her throat, Ruth realized that if they were spotted now, they would be taken back too.

"Look out for the bridge," said Edek.

3

He and Jan shot ahead, aiming for the center of the three arches. Edging away from the square, Ruth paddled towards the right-hand arch. Edek's canoe shot under the arch and disappeared into the shadows. Too far to the right, Ruth got caught in sluggish water. She drifted broadside on to the base of the arch. She paddled frantically to get free, but the canoe was still across the base of the arch, with the water thrusting against each end, threatening to break its back. She jabbed hard with the paddle and managed to ease it a little. With a last effort she thrust at the stonework and the canoe broke free. The canoe swung sideways into the shadows under the arch, then shot out

4

Ruth peered ahead to see if she could see anything of the other canoe. Then the moon went behind a cloud and the darkness hid her.

On and on they sped, the water foaming against the bows, spitting and bubbling against the canvas.

"I'm sitting in the river," said Bronia but Ruth took no notice. "Edek! Jan!" she shouted.

5

As they rounded a bend, they were thrust towards the right bank. The river was quieter here and soon they felt the bottom of the canoe scrape over pebbles and slow them to a halt. Ruth put her hand over the side and down into the water and tried to shove them off but they were stuck. There was a pale light in the sky now, and the rim of the hills stood out dark against it. It was still too dark to see much, but she could make out rocks in the water, rounded like hippos' backs.

"We'll have to get out and push," she said.

6

They stepped into the water, which was little more than ankle deep, and at once the canoe floated. With the painter in her hand and Bronia beside her, she drew it gently along till they came to a large V-shaped rock that seemed to project from the bank. She pulled the canoe high and dry onto a shoal of pebbles, then lifted Bronia onto a rock.

7

"We must wait here till daylight," she said.

And they sat there shivering and clinging to each other till the shadows brightened and they could see the whole sweep of the river, white and broken in the middle, rock-strewn and shallow at either side, with the wood-muffled hills hemming it in, and not a soul in sight. No sign of Edek and Jan. They could not have felt lonelier.

8

They turned the canoe over and poured water out. Stepping aboard, they headed for midstream. And the current caught them and carried them on towards the rapids.

The river grew faster and the bank flashed past. Soon they were in a kind of gorge, where the river squeezed past great boulders, some of them as high as houses. Some of the swells were over a foot high, and the spray dashed over the bow and stung their faces. The water roared here so that even the loudest shout could not be heard. Out to the left there were huge oily surges that looked as if they would pound you down into the depths if you got caught in them.

9

Bronia closed her eyes and clung to her sister's waist. Ruth was not as scared as she had expected to be. With a triumphant sense of exhilaration she flashed in with her paddle, heading always for the open stream, away from the white broken water where the rocks lay hidden. Now and then a boulder loomed up and she knew that if they struck it they would be dashed to pieces. But a quick dip of the paddle at the right moment was enough to shoot them safely past. In no time the river broadened, the boulders eased and the banks were wooded again. The terrors of the rapids were over.

10

Ruth hoped that Edek and Jan, whose two-seater was much less easy to maneuver, had been as successful as they had. There seemed no need for the paddle now, for the water was clear of rocks and the current smooth and swift. They could lie back and let the canoe take care of itself.

Bronia closed her eyes and fell asleep. Ruth lay back and watched the blue sky overhead and the climbing sun. It was to be another scorching day, and she too became sleepy and dozed.

11

We hope you will feel ready to try to read the rest of this exciting book. Remember reading is a skill and will only improve if you practice. The choice is yours, so explore your local library or school library or bookstore. You are certain to find something that interests you. Discover the pleasure of finding a "good read" and do just that!

READ, READ, READ!

12

Higher dictionary skills

You are probably already quite familiar with your dictionary. You have learned the quartiles: A-D; E-M; N-R; S-Z which help you find words quickly. You are now ready to explore your dictionary more fully.

1. Listen to the teacher. (See page 21.) Start your dictionary exploration by reading the introduction. This will tell you how your dictionary functions, i.e., how it is organized and how words are presented. Topics covered will include: pronunciation, i.e., phonetics and accent; usage, i.e., grammar and origins of words. The words in **bold** at the top of each page are always the **first** and the **last** word on that page.

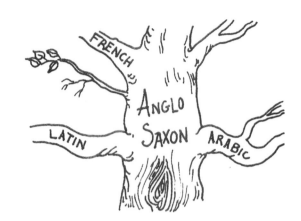

etymology n. the account of, facts relating to, formation and meaning of a word; the branch of linguistic science concerned with the part of grammar dealing with individual words and their formations and inflections.

2. What abbreviations does your dictionary use for **noun**, **verb**, **adjective**, and **adverb**?

3. Use your dictionary to complete the table.

Noun	Verb	Adjective	Adverb
action	act	active	actively
			educationally
	philosophize		
			explosively
		visual	
wonder			
	fly		
		laughable	

4. Write definitions for these words to show their different meanings:

cybernetics   dolmen   infusion   nous   quiescent   undulating

Successful spelling!
The last few bricks in the construction

1. To stop **e i y** from making the letter **g** soft, (giant, gentle, gypsy) we insert the letter **u** as a / wall. This keeps the **g** hard (gun **g**). Read (but don't sound the **u**).

		guideline	rogue	guest	beguile	guillotine
guy	guiltless	guess	vague	catalogue	guitar	guinea
guilty	guidance	plague	tongue	disguise	guild	pig

2. Words ending in **ce** and **ge** must keep the **e** so that **c** and **g** remain soft.

   Example: notice + able = noticeable   service + able = serviceable
   manage + able = manageable   courage + ous = courageous

   Sometimes to keep the previous vowel long the **e** remains.
   sale saleable   rate rateable

3. Words commonly misused:
   - aggravate - to make worse
   - irritate - to annoy or exasperate
   - beside - at the side of
   - besides - in addition to
   - astronomy - study of the planets and stars
   - astrology - foretelling the future by the stars
   - compare - to point out similarities
   - contrast - to point out differences

4. Words commonly misspelled
   - all right
   - separate
   - practice   - **noun**
   - to practice - **verb**
   - vacuum
   - proceed   **but** procedure
   - quite   - somewhat
   - quiet   - without noise

5. This is another group of words where the **u** is silent: build   building   built   builder

   These, too, are tricky spellings. busy   business

6. Find a word in the sections above to fit the definitions below.

   1. Another word for a company. _____

   2. A finding of the court, incurring a penalty. _____

   3. Involved in the construction industry. _____

   4. There is great excitement in the world of _____ at the discovery of a new star.

   5. He could _____ his skin condition by using certain detergents.

   6. It is good _____ to _____ for twenty minutes every day.

   7. It is _____ difficult to keep a baby _____ in church.

   8. Don't _____ me when I am trying to study.

Wonders and wondering

What is the meaning of the verb to wonder?
The dictionary defines it as: to have a feeling of admiration; to marvel at; to think about with curiosity.
This is how wonder is listed in the thesaurus in the Franklin Wordmaster:

Nouns		Verbs	
admiration	curiosity	ask oneself	question
astonishment	marvel	conjecture	speculate
awe	miracle	inquire	think
bewilderment	portent	meditate	boggle
curiosity	prodigy	ponder	gape
fascination	rarity	puzzle	gawk
surprise	sight	query	marvel
	spectacle		stare

Do you ever stop and wonder about things? Do you take time to marvel and admire? Young children are always actively curious (which can lead them into danger if they are not carefully watched).

Ancient Wonders

These are known as the seven wonders of the ancient world. They are:
The Colossus of Rhodes
The Pharos at Alexandria
The Hanging Gardens of Babylon
The Temple of Artemis at Ephesus
The Pyramids of Giza
The Tomb of Mausolus at Halicarnassus
The Statue of Zeus at Olympia

Find out as much as you can about each of these and then see if you can answer these questions in your exercise book:

1. What do these wonders have in common?
2. Could you visit "The Hanging Gardens of Babylon?"
3. Where is Giza?
4. What is a "pharos?"
5. Who was Zeus?
6. What is a colossus?

Natural wonders

Have you heard of the Victoria Falls? The Africans call them "Mosi oa Tunya" or "The Smoke that Thunders." They are more than 1 mile (1600m) wide and 335 feet (102m) deep. Other incredible natural wonders of the world include: the Grand Canyon – a deep chasm in northwest Arizona; Mount Everest; and the northern lights.

Find out as much as you can about these natural wonders and then answer these questions in your exercise book:

1. What are the dimensions of the Grand Canyon? How was it formed?
2. Who named the Victoria Falls?
3. Where is Mount Everest?

   Who were the first two men to climb to the summit of Everest?
4. What are the northern lights?

   What causes this phenomenon?

MODERN WONDERS
What would you consider to be the wonders of the world of this modern age or your lifetime? Complete the mindmap.

You may want to use some of these ideas or you may have plenty of your own:
transplant surgery; nuclear power; the laser beam; genetic engineering.

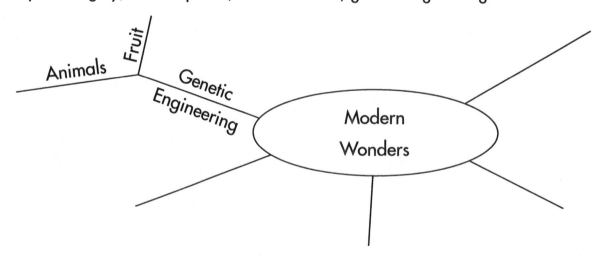

1. What do you think your great grandparents would have considered to be the wonders of their time?
2. What do you think the wonders of this millennium will be? Draw a mindmap of these.
3. I hope this has made you marvel at the wonders of life. Look for the miracles in your midst: the development of a human being from a single cell; the growth of a huge oak tree from a small acorn; the stars in the universe and the dawning of each new day.

Certificate of Merit

presented to

_____

for the successful completion of

Reading Success Book 6

Signed _____

Teacher

Date _____

Appendix A

Reading and Sound Cards

ie	IE	-sion	-SION
oi	OI	aw	AW
oy	OY	ew	EW
ur	UR	au	AU

chief **E**

pie **I**

coin **o y**

boy **o y**

nurse **e r**

procession **s h 'n**

television **z h 'n**

claw **aw**

stew **U**

crew **oo**

sauce **aw**

-ear / -EAR	ar / AR
-cian / -CIAN	ei / EI
-ous / -OUS	ou / OU
-ue / -UE	or / OR

Appendix A
Reading Pack
Vowels and vowel consonant digraphs—Book 6—Sheet 2—Back **(pink paper)**

earth	bear	ear
e r	**A** → **A r**	**E** → **E r**
magician		
s h' n		
	collar	mars
	ə r	**a r**
	ceiling	weight
	E	**A**
dangerous		
U **s**		
	soup	couple	house
	oo	**u**	**ow**
argue	glue		
U	**oo**		
	doctor	fort
	ə r	**o r**

Appendix A
Sound Pictures/Spelling Pack
Vowels and vowel consonant digraphs—Book 6—Sheet 3—Front **(pink paper)**

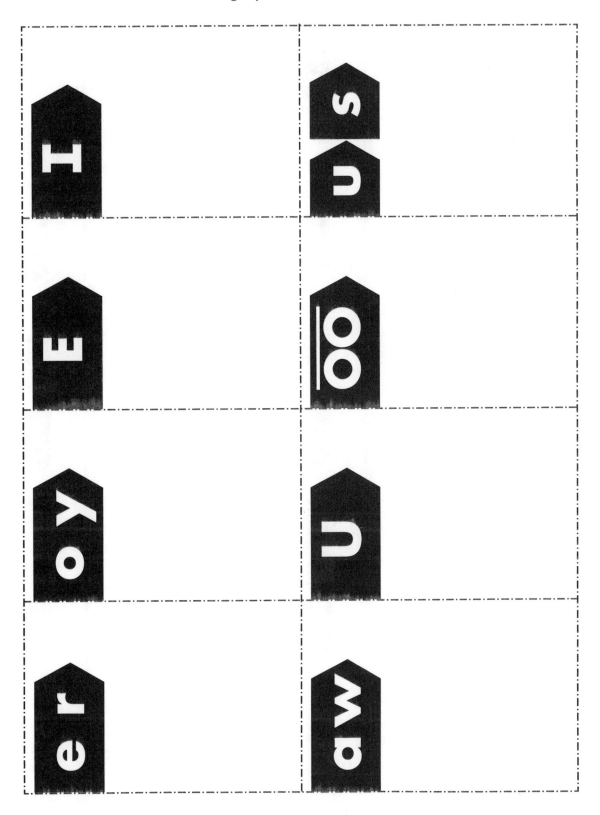

Appendix A

Reading & Sound Pictures/Spelling Pack
Vowels and vowel consonant digraphs—Book 6—Sheet 3—Back **(pink paper)**

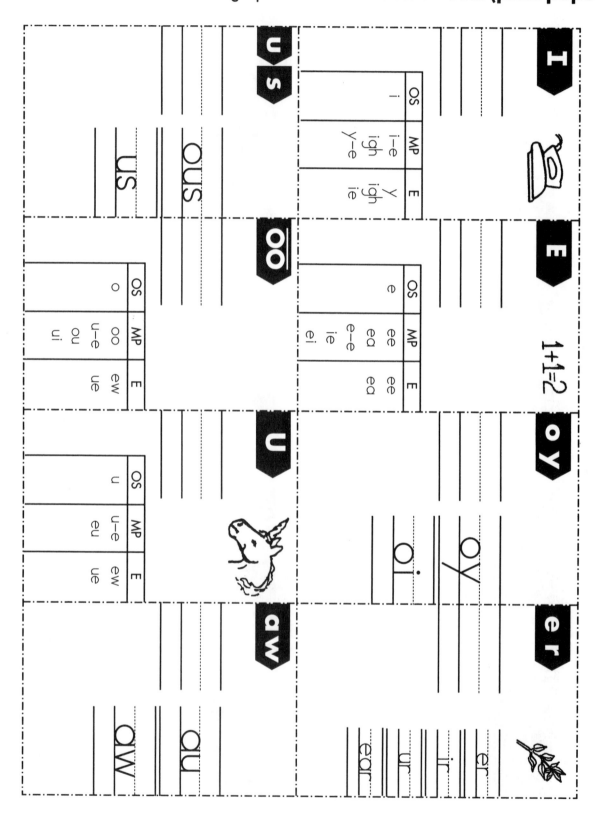

y-e

Y-E

A

o

u

zh'n

er

sh'n

-oe

-OE

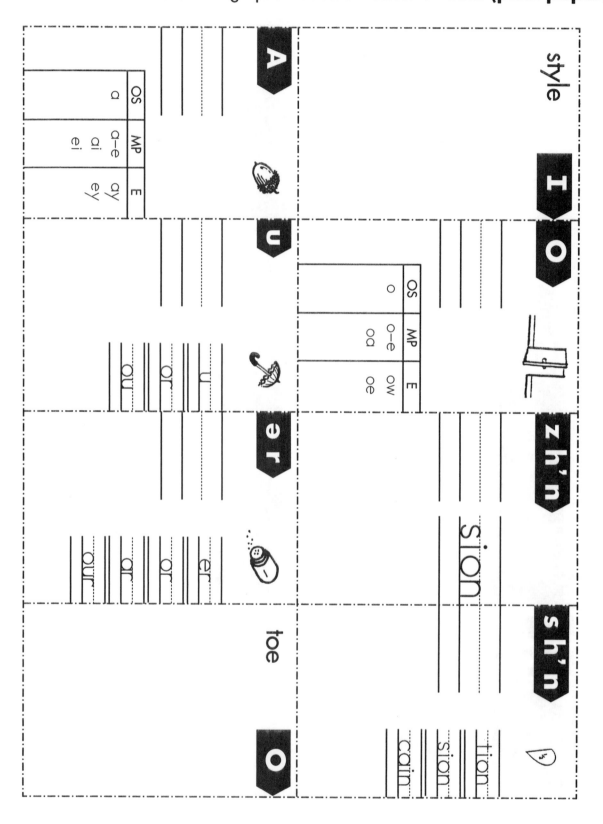

f

k

s h

ch

CH

ph

PH

-que

-QUE

Appendix A
Sound Pictures/Spelling Pack
Consonants and consonant digraphs—Book 6—Sheet 5—Back (green paper)

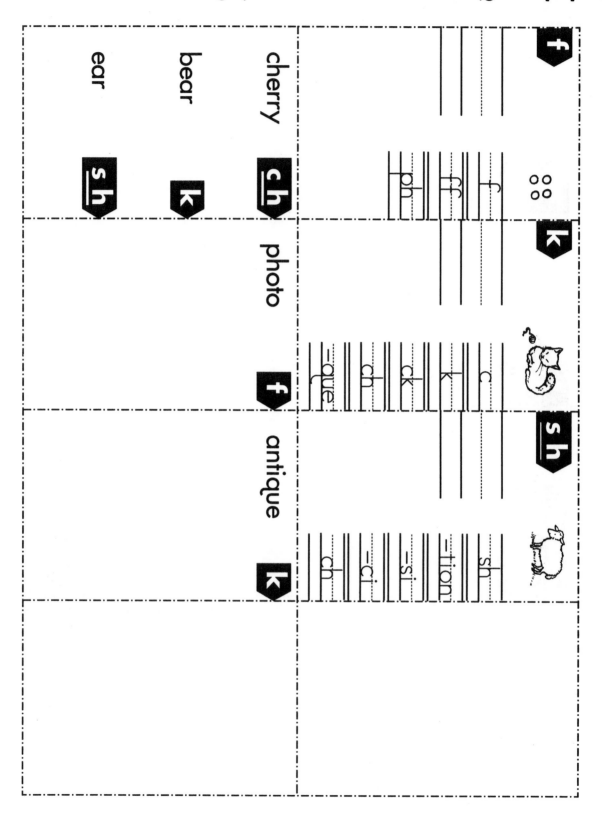

The Long Vowel Choices Chart

Long Vowel Sound Picture	Open Syllable	Main part of word				End of word		
		1st try	2nd try	3rd try	4th try	1st try	2nd try	3rd try

The Long Vowel Choices Chart

Long Vowel Sound Picture	Open Syllable	Main part of word 1st try	Main part of word 2nd try	Main part of word 3rd try	Main part of word 4th try	End of word 1st try	End of word 2nd try	End of word 3rd try
A	a (v c v) acorn	a–e cake	ai tail	ei weight	ei reindeer	ay tray	ey grey	
E	e (v c v) equals	ee queen	ea cream	e–e athlete	ie chief	ee bee	ea tea	
I	i (v c v) iron	i–e smile	igh right	y–e style		y cry	igh high	ie pie
O	o (v c v) open	o–e nose	oa goat			ow snow	oe toe	
U	u (v c v) uniform	u–e tube	eu Europe			ew stew	ue argue	
OO	ru (v c v) ruby	oo spoon	u–e rule	ou soup		ew crew	ue glue	

LL80106 *Reading Success Book 6*

Long Vowel Chart Puzzle Pieces
Can you put them in the correct places?

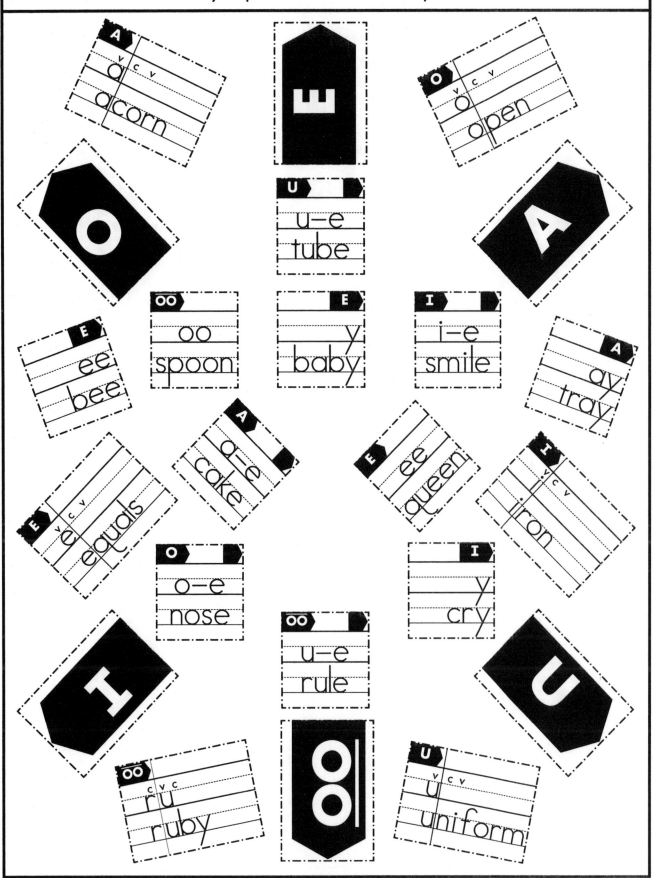

Long Vowel Chart Puzzle Pieces
Can you put them in the correct places?

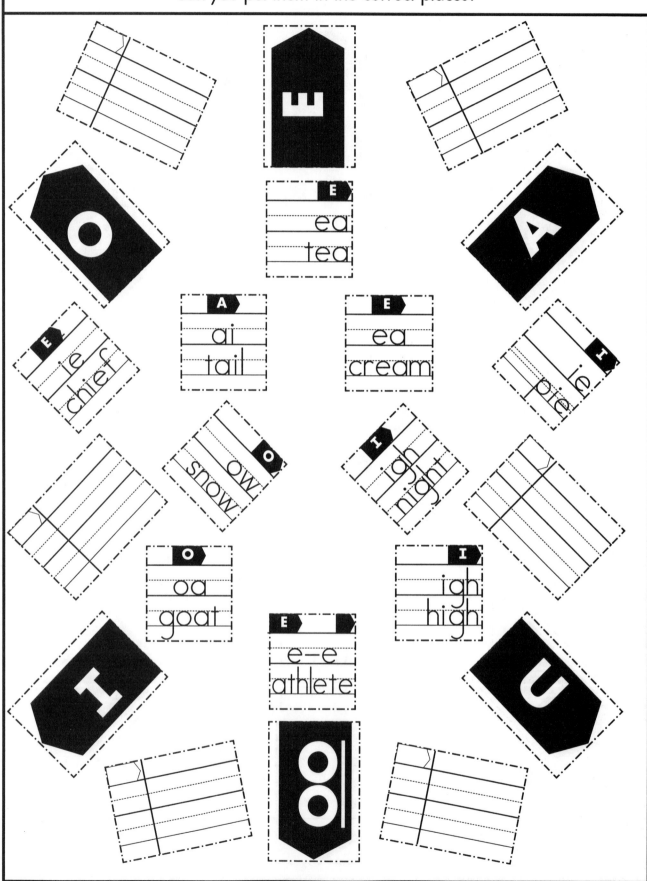

Long Vowel Chart Puzzle Pieces
Can you put them in the correct places?

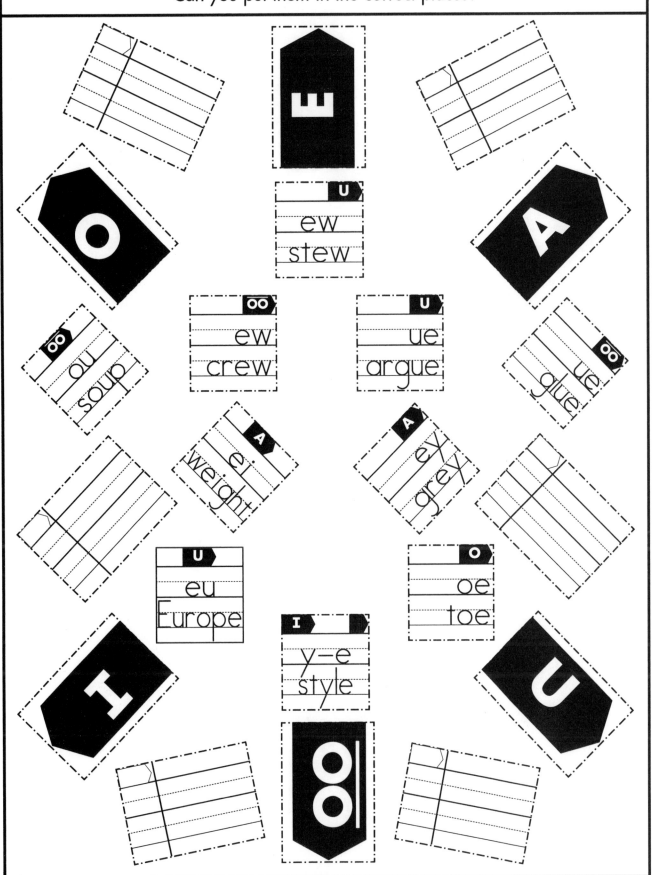

Lists of Words to be Used as Flash Cards for Sentence Building

Vowel Pattern ur

hurt
fur
urban
church
turn
turban
burp
burst
surplus
burn
curl
burden
curb
absurd
nurse
disturb
Thursday
curve
return
purse
spurn
gurgle
murderer
surf
surge

Vowel Pattern oy

boy
coy
employ
annoy
oyster
convoy
toy
soy
joy
destroy
decoy
enjoy
alloy

Vowel Pattern oi

broil
oil
join
moist
coil
noise
soil
joint
boil
choice
toil
spoil
void
coin
sirloin
foil
joist
rejoice
turmoil
anoint
ointment
voice
turquoise
tabloid
Polaroid
point
appointment

Long Vowel Pattern ie (E)

shield
chief
field
believe
priest
thief
niece
cashier
yield
brief
fierce
diesel
pier
pierce
siege
shriek
belief
thieves
niece
masterpiece
reprieve
briefcase

Long Vowel Pattern ie (I)

die
tie
pie
lie
fie
magpies
vie
untie
died
flies
skies
cries

Vowel Digraph Pattern au

sauce
taut
haul
maul
fault
cause
pause
launch
faucet
fraud
haunts
gaunt
flaunt
paunch
pause
gauze
vault
because
caused
autumn
laundry
gaudy
fauna
applause
traumatic
inaudible
authority
jaundice

Consonant Digraph ph

phone
trophy
photo
graph
phonics
prophet
phase
dolphin
phony
phrase
gopher
elephant
orphan
phantom
pamphlet
typhoon
hyphen
phrase
sphinx
aphid
physics
lymph
phobia
pharmacy
emphasis
pheasant
sapphire
autobiography
hemisphere
amphibian
prophet
telegraph
philosophy
graph
geography
microphone
alphabet
atmosphere
metamorphosis
demography
biography

Long Vowel Pattern ew

pew
stew
few
new
dew
knew
chew
screw
crew
brew
threw
drew
flew
grew
jewel
pewter
cashew
sewer
mildew
nephew
curfew
screwdriver
Hebrew
slew

Vowel Digraph Pattern aw

law
jaw
claw
raw
paw
thaw
straw
shawl
yawn
crawl
brawl
lawn
awning
squawk
fawn
draw
drawl
straw
awful
saw

flaw
sprawl
pawn
withdraw
strawberry
dawdle
crawling
sawdust
awkward
coleslaw
unlawful
hawthorn
sprawling

Syllable Pattern -sion

mansion
commission
convulsion
pension
extension
confession
passion
suspension
admission
tension
transmission
suppression
adhesion
profusion
version
illusion
conclusion
occasion
division
revision
dimension
expansion

Long Vowel Pattern ue

glue
clue
sue
due
true
hue
rescue
endue
virtue
pursue

value
blue
continue
avenue
revenue
barbecue

Words with Silent Letters

lamb
tomb
limb
numb
crumb
dumb
plumber
comb
knob
kneel
knock
knocker
knocking
knee
knit
knew
knight
know
knowledge
knelt
calf
talk
half
walk
stalk
folk
yolk
balm
gnat
gnu
gnash
sign
signing
resign
signed
ensign
campaign
wrote
written
wreck
wrap

wriggle
wrong
wring
wreath

Vowel Suffix -ous

serious
generous
pompous
various
jealous
continuous
nervous
fabulous
numerous
famous
humorous
marvelous
ridiculous
poisonous
treacherous
venomous
tremendous
adventurous
courteous
spontaneous
hideous
miscellaneous
erroneous
sumptuous
contemptuous

Nouns Ending with us

crocus
Pegasus
genius
focus
bonus
Fergus
sinus
Venus
virus
citrus
exodus
cactus
octopus
chorus
campus
hippopotamus

Consonant Digraph ch (K)

echo
ache
orchestra
orchid
chord
chrome
chronic
anchor
school
Christmas
scheme
chorus
schedule
monarch
lichen
charismatic
character
chlorine
bronchitis
melancholy
chaos
chronicle
chasm
chord
mechanic

Consonant Digraph ch (sh)

chivalry
chalet
parachute
Chicago
machine
avalanche
chiffon
chaise
brochure
moustache
chevron
chandelier
chauffeur
chute
eustachian
Charlotte

Introducing -que

antique
technique
unique
plaque
oblique
grotesque

Syllable Pattern -cian

magician
technician
obstetrician
physician
optician
electrician
beautician
dietician
politician
mathematician

Final Syllables -el, -al, -le

dabble
tinkle
pimple
rattle
mingle
handle
dangle
bristles
stable
temple
Bible
single
ankle
mangle
shuttle
angel
cancel
Nigel
Angela
marcel
parcel
triangle
novel
dimple
chancel
gravel
fictional

additional
medal
Abel
meddle

Vowel Pattern ear

rear
dear
near
spear
gear
fearfully
hearing
earn
pearl
early
search
dearth
yearned
learned
Earl
heard
shear
year
tear
dreary
cleared
beard
feared
reared
sheared
neared
clearing
appeared
disappeared

Reading: -ti, -ci, -ssi, -xi say (sh)

provincial
commercial
position
torrential
noxious
patience
ancient
suspicious
officious
sufficient
superficial

malicious
facial
passion
permission
crucial
auspicious
efficient
superstitious
influential
ferocious
cautious
patient

Suffix -or (or)

actor
cursor
tutor
supervisor
tractor
factor
advisor
calculator
sponsor
juror
author
indicator
anchor
motor
ambassador
bachelor
janitor
director
born
short
absorb
torment
morsel
ancestor
organ
dictator
equator

Suffix -or (er)

worm
worker
worst
work
world
worth
word
wormy

worthy
wording
worry
worse
wordy
worship
worsen

Vowel Pattern ou with Different Sounds

soup
group
toucan
youth
croup
goulash
croutons
troupe
uncouth
wound

Long Vowel Pattern eigh and ei (A)

weight
eight
eighteen
neighbor
eighty
sleigh
weigh
veil
skein
rein
seine
veil
reigns
surveillance
feign

Long Vowel Pattern ei (E)

receipt
receive
deceive
receiver
conceit
conceive
perceive

deceit
caffeine
seizure
leisure
protein
inveigle
neither
either
Neil
weird
seize
Sheila
sheik

Vowel Digraph ey and irregular sound ey (E) and (A)

donkey
monkey
parsley
chimney
pulley
whiskey
kidney
trolley
honey
jockey
barley
turkey
journey
they
grey
disobey
prey
survey
convey
obey
whey

Suffix -ar

beggar
dollar
cedar
lunar
collar
pillar
popular
nectar
polar

grammar
cellar
solar
muscular
vulgar
similar
rectangular
scholar
calendar
altar

Vowel Digraphs eu, ui, and oe

feud
neurologist
Eucharist
Eunice
neutral
neurology
neuter
heuristic
neuron
pneumonia
maneuver
euthenics
eulogy
eureka
Teutonic
therapeutic
euthanasia
deuce
euphemism
Europe
pharmaceutical
fruit
suit
bruise
suitcase
cruise
juice
Joe
hoe
toe
doe
roe
flow
sloe
aloe
foe
throes

tiptoe
mistletoe
oboe

Difficult Words to Spell
purpose
scissors
business
possess
success
accident
library
accommodation
language
bicycle
certificate
genuine
decision
special
separate
vehicle
valuable
frequent

Conjunctions
and
if
although
but
because
when
unless
so
or
and

Adverbs
swiftly
easily
slowly
safely
neatly
lazily
skillfully
clumsily
carefully
eventually
intently
craftily
cunningly

bravely
attentively
actively
creatively
constructively
responsively
thoughtfully
icily
competitively
beautifully
explosively
deceptively
imaginatively
photographically
inventively
falsely
threateningly
sensitively
conversationally
characteristically
descriptively
resentfully
spectacularly
destructively

Adjectives
active
creative
constructive
thoughtful
responsive
icy
competitive
beautiful
explosive
deceptive
imaginative
inventive
falsified
threatening
sensational
conversational
descriptive
resentful

Verbs
to act
to create
to think
to respond
to divide
to ice
to compete
to beautify
to explode
to deceive
to imagine
to photograph
to invent
to falsify
to threaten
to sense
to converse
to characterize
to describe
to resent
to receive
to destroy

Prepositions
with
between
below
in
across
behind
on
through
from
over
under
near

Pronouns
you
I
who
she
he
her
him
everyone
me
it
they
them

Math Words
acute
area
angle
average
circumference
coordinate
compass
consecutive
degree
denominator
diameter
equation
equilateral
graph
hypotenuse
integers
isosceles
kilometer
millimeter
numerator
numbers
obtuse
perimeter
perpendicular
product
protractor
radius
ratio
right angle
scalene
square
sum
triangle

Science Words
acid
alkali
neutralize
chlorophyll
molecule
evaporation
gravity
distillation
catalyst
base
organism
electrolysis
reduction
displacement
photosynthesis
diffusion
decomposition
element
oxidation
genes

Notes...

Notes...

Notes...

Notes...

Notes...

Notes...